W9-AUD-176

Acknowledgments

Special thanks go to the many people who helped make this book possible: My clients and students who let me know what was needed. Mary Lou Andersen, Lyn Greenleaf James and Janet McCrary for proof reading and suggestions. Brian Templeton for his insightful, entertaining editorial comments. MK Valett for her final edits. Jerrold Jenkins, Bobbie Hurst, Jan Nathan and Pamela Woodward for peer reviews and Mary Westheimer of the BookZone, for her expertise with the Internet. And Mom, for inspiring independence.

*Dedicated to those who
bring their message to the world.*

A Simple Guide to **Marketing** Your Book

What An Author And Publisher Can Do To Sell More Books

A WISE OWL BOOK

www.wiseowlbooks.com/publish

A Simple Guide to Marketing Your Book
Copyright © 1998, 2001 by Mark Ortman
All rights reserved

3 4 5 6 7 8 / 2003 2002

Revised Edition 2001

ISBN 0-9634699-4-0

Manufactured in the United States of America by Bang Printing, Brainerd, MN

Cover Design: Lanphear Design, Snohomish, WA

WISE OWL BOOKS • Box 29205 • Bellingham WA 98228 • USA • (360) 671-5858

Wesite: http://www.wiseowlbooks.com/publish

Publisher's Cataloging in Publication

Ortman, Mark
A simple guide to marketing your book: what an author
and publisher can do to sell more books / [Mark Ortman] --
1st ed.
p. cm.
Includes index.
Preassigned LCCN: 97-62447
ISBN: 0-9634699-4-0

1. Books--Marketing. 2. Selling--Books 3. Publishers
and publishing. I. Title.

Z471.078 1998   381.450'02
                                         QBI97-41621

Contents

Introduction

Marketing a book is a creative task filled with decisions about distribution, publicity and promotion. This book will make many of those decisions easier. Since no one can accurately predict the commercial success of a book, the only way to find out is to give your book its best chance to succeed with the least risk. As with any product, this requires testing, planning and promotion.

The best time to start your marketing program is well before your book is printed. Reduce your financial risk by **test marketing** your book idea. Share your manuscript with peers and members of your target audience, ask for honest assessment and listen carefully to the reaction. Interview other authors and publishers on what it takes to be successful. Their suggestions may inspire ideas for your own book. Consider writing an article about your book's message and submit it to appropriate magazines for publication. Responses to your article can be the start of a good mailing list and help assess the quantity of books to print initially. Pre-sell and begin testing the demand 2-9 months before the publication date.

In addition to a great title and a professional cover design, the most effective way to sell books is with a marketing plan. With so many options available to the author/publisher, it is easy to become overwhelmed. A marketing plan outlines suitable ways to reach readers in the most efficient and economic manner.

The purpose of this book is to guide you through the planning process by explaining in an instructive manner *how to get started, where to find the best places to distribute your book* and the *many ways to create a demand through publicity and promotion.* Whether you are author or publisher, or both, using this handbook will save time by leading you to many industry resources that can help with your book marketing campaign.

This book is filled with checklists, resources and cost-saving ideas, organized into four chapters: Developing Your Book's Marketing Plan, Book Distribution, Publicity and Ways To Sell Your Books Direct. There is an appendix and an index with resources and references to make your book marketing effort easier. Request information from the many organizations listed, as they provide other useful services beyond the pages of this book. Internet addresses have been included where available.

To get the most from this book, read each chapter before preparing your marketing plan. Then, buy a notebook and retreat to a quiet place to compile your list of people, places and publications to pursue. This book will guide you through the process. The time you spend developing a thorough plan will save you from inertia and missed selling opportunities. Your marketing plan is the foundation and compass to navigate a successful book selling campaign.

As we bring our message to the world, we have a chance to inform, entertain and influence the hearts and minds of many. The possibilities of far-reaching recognition and financial reward make marketing a book a creative and exciting endeavor. Good luck!

Mark Ortman

It's easy to get where you're going.
Just define wherever you want to be
as where you intend to go.

1. Developing Your Book's Marketing Plan

Book Marketing is the task of identifying who would find value in reviewing, reselling and buying your book. The marketing plan outlines the steps to achieve this aim and involves researching and selecting appropriate avenues to meet your book's sales objectives. Promotion, on the other hand, has to do with creating the demand. The marketing and promotion of a book is as unique as the author who wrote it, thus each title requires its own plan.

If your marketing campaign is carefully researched, wisely planned and relentlessly executed, it will fare much better than optimistically waiting for your book to sell on its own. More than 150,000 titles are published in the United States each year. A strong marketing and promotional effort is the *only* chance to gain attention in such a crowded arena. In developing a marketing plan, recognize the lag time between your efforts and the responses as some avenues have a short sales cycle and others much longer. Test various strategies to see what will work best for you, your book and your cash flow. Develop your marketing plan several months in advance (ideally, 3-9 months for a national release) to allow for the long lead times and submission requirements of many distribution and promotional possibilities. The objective of your marketing effort must be clear and focused, yet flexible enough to accommodate new opportunities. A marketing plan evolves. Make periodic adjustments to include discoveries you have made along the way. Your book's marketing campaign is a sustained effort over time. Like pushing a snowball up a hill, you're never quite certain when it will top the summit and begin rolling on its own.

Components of Your Marketing Plan

Planning is essential to the success of your book. With so many alternatives available to the author/publisher, a clearly written marketing plan is the best way to maximize your efforts. It is the compass for a productive book-selling campaign and a requirement for many distribution channels. Following are the key components to a marketing plan. (*See page 84 for a blank Marketing Plan Questionnaire worksheet.*)

Components of your marketing plan are:

1. **Budget:** How much do I spend?
2. **Product:** What am I selling?
3. **Audience:** Who will buy it and where can they be found?
4. **Distribution:** How and where will my book be made available?
5. **Promotion:** What will be done to create a demand for my book?
6. **Timing:** When will the plan be implemented?

Plan your work, then work your plan.

1. Budget (HOW much to spend?)

Plan a budget well in advance of promoting your book. Then, decisions about what you *want* and what you can *afford* will be easier. A general guideline for a marketing budget is: $.50 to $1.00 per book, depending upon the quantity printed. Then, set aside 10 to 15% of net sales for ongoing promotion. How the budget is allocated is influenced by the book, the audience and the most cost-effective ways to reach them. Throwing money at risky promotional activities adds up quickly, chipping away at a book's profit. Cash flow problems are not uncommon in publishing. Most conventional channels of distribution pay 90-120 days later. This is why so many authors/publishers invest more time pursuing secondary channels of distribution, which offer much shorter payment terms. Accurately predicting the success of a book is difficult. Anticipate the unexpected by having a cash reserve budgeted for reprints. Most marketing expenses will go toward:

- Postage & Supplies
- Review Copy Giveaways
- Printed Promotional Matter
- Advertising
- Travel / Touring
- Miscellaneous (Education and Consulting)

Where does each dollar go after a book is published? Below is a general breakdown of expenses based upon a percentage of the **retail price** of the book:

- Re-Printing   10-15%
- Distribution   0-65% (depending on the channel used)
- Author Royalty   5-10%
- Ongoing Promotion   10-15%
- Overhead & Profit   20-35%

Publishing is a complicated business with many variables. The profitability of a book is established by managing expenses against sales. Weigh each expenditure in view of the potential long and short term sales gain. It is also a risky business. Of every ten books published, three earn a profit, four break even and the rest lose money. Profit can be especially elusive for slow moving books, so it's important to treat your book selling venture as a business.

Business is something which,
if you don't have any, you go out of.

2. Product (WHAT are you selling?)

Instead of thinking you are selling a book, look at it as selling a message. If people like your message, they will buy your book. Typically, people are looking for something newer, better or easier. Translate your book's message so as to meet your audience's needs. Compile a list of key selling points to use in promotional materials and advertising copy. Find that unique twist or angle to your topic, particularly if other books have been written on the same subject. In other words, differentiate your book from similar ones on the market. This helps to attract attention when presenting to reviewers, the media, your audience and various distribution channels.

Your audience is interested in your book because of what your book will do for them. This is the book's "benefits". Features (facts) describe the book, whereas benefits sell the book. Capture your audience's interest by promoting the book's benefits. The following questions will help define and clarify your book's benefits and sales message, and provide useful dialogue when conducting media interviews and other promotional activities.

- What is the main message or theme running through your book?
- Why is that message or theme important?
- In one paragraph describe what your book is about.
- How is it unique from other books on the same or similar subjects?
- What are the realistic strengths and weaknesses of your book?
- By reading your book, what benefit will the reader:

    - Gain?
    - Save?
    - Do?
    - Become?

- Write an author's biography (written in the third person).

The author can be just as marketable as the book; sometimes more so. The purpose of the author's biography is to humanize the author and establish credibility in the eyes of the reader. Include:

- Why the book was written.
- The biggest lesson learned relating to this book's subject.
- Education and professional training.
- Prizes, honors and awards earned.
- Memberships in professional associations, clubs and organizations.
- Specific qualifications for writing this book.
- Circumstances connected with the book that might have news value.

> The broader and more general the subject of a book, the more it will cost to market and promote to your audience.

3. Audience (WHO will buy your book and WHERE can they be found?)

Typically, there are multiple audiences for a book. The sooner you recognize, isolate, and locate the people or organizations most likely to be interested in your book, the more money you can save reaching them. Some books have a clearly defined and obvious market, while the market for other books may be quite broad. Nearly every industry or market niche has at least one association, magazine or newsletter devoted to it. One technique that helps to identify *who* will buy your book and *where* to find them, is compiling a list of occupations, organizations, associations, opinion leaders, hobbyists, friends or anyone you can think of who would want to own your book. Divide the list into actual versus prospective customers. Then, list those you want to reach first, second, third, etc. Review the list to see if there is any overlap geographically, demographically or through membership interests. This will help you direct your promotional efforts efficiently and give you insight into *where* and *how* to best reach your audience. In the end, tracking sales will define *who, how* and *where* people buy your book, providing valuable information to direct and adjust future marketing efforts.

- Who would benefit from the information in your book?
- List the key opinion leaders on the subject of your book.
- To which associations or clubs might the reader belong?
- What conferences or conventions might they attend?
- Which catalogs might they receive by mail?
- Where do they shop or hang out?
- What media formats do they read, watch and listen to?
- Which companies, organizations, associations could use your book as a premium or giveaway?

Familiarize yourself with the following publications found at the reference desk in the library. These are resources to help identify and locate your audience and are referred to throughout this book.

- Directories in Print by Gale Group

- Guide to American Directories by Todd Publications

- Standard Directory of Periodicals

- Oxbridge Directory of Newsletters

- Directory of Mail Order Catalogs

- Oxbridge National Directory of Catalogs

- Thomas Register of American Manufacturers

- Brands And Their Companies, A Gale Trade Names Directory

- Directory of Premium, Incentive & Travel Buyers

- Encyclopedia of Associations

- Trade Show Worldwide by Gale Group

- Directory of Publications & Broadcast Media

- Gebbie's All in One Directory

- American Book Trade Directory by R.R. Bowker

- Literary Market Place

- Contemporary Authors

- Chase's Annual Events Directory

4. Distribution   (WHERE will your book be made available?)

After targeting your audience, what will be the most appropriate and efficient means to reach them? Your goal is to establish numerous distribution options instead of relying on just one. Even with an exclusive distribution arrangement, there are often many secondary markets the author/publisher can pursue which won't overlap or conflict. Build your distribution network by selling your book through as many channels as possible.

- Where are books similar to yours being sold?
- Who could sell your book along with their product or service?
- Where can you make your book available to the reader?

❏ Associations	❏ Government
❏ Book Clubs	❏ Internet
❏ Bookstores	❏ Libraries
❏ Catalogs	❏ Premiums and Incentives
❏ Corporations	❏ Specialty Retail Outlets
❏ Foreign Markets	❏ TV Shopping Networks
❏ Fundraisers	❏ Warehouse Clubs

When working with a modest budget, reach your market in the most cost-efficient manner. Find the best fits between distribution and your audience. Allow the sales from one area to finance the growth into another area. Included in the cost of distribution are discounts given and the price of persuading vendors to carry your book. Not everyone will be interested in stocking your title. Stay with your plan long enough to profit and be aware of the lag time between effort, sales and income.

Publicity and promotion **must** support distribution. If your marketing plan includes sales through conventional channels of distribution (bookstores & libraries), a second sale must be made to their suppliers. For example; most bookstores prefer buying through a wholesaler or distributor as this simplifies their ordering procedure with one-stop shopping and billing. In addition to a marketable book and a publicity minded author, a well conceived marketing plan is the most persuasive tool a publisher has to influence a distributor's or wholesaler's stocking decision. Stocking decisions are based on sales potential. Continually ask yourself if the cost to obtain distribution in each channel exceeds the potential return. Is this the most efficient means of reaching your audience?

5. Promotion (WHAT will be done to create a demand?)

What are you going to do to let the reader know about your book and where to buy it? Relying on distribution channels to do all the selling is a mistake. It is up to the author/publisher to create the demand though publicity and promotion. Design an inventive or daring promotional strategy for each market segment you are trying to reach. Then decide how each idea will be implemented. There are six ways to reach people through your promotional efforts: direct mail, fax, internet, the media (print and electronic), advertising and personal appearances. Realize that not everyone will respond to the same medium; each promotional idea takes innovation and creativity by matching the book's sales message with the audience. Research, instinct, costs, your book and trial and error will decide which medium is best to use.

- What will be done to publicize your book?

❏ Book Reviews	❏ Targeted book giveaways
❏ Media Appearances	❏ Submit articles to the print media

- What will be done to sell and create a demand for your book?

❏ Advertise	❏ Internet
❏ Author Tour	❏ Presentations / Personal Appearances
❏ Direct Mail	❏ Trade Shows

- Who can you ask to endorse or provide a testimonial?

6. Timing (WHEN will the ideas be implemented?)

When are the Trade and the Reader in their most favorable buying moods? Does your book have a seasonal theme? Publishers release books throughout the year, but focus on Spring and Fall. Readers purchase year-round with an emphasis on the holiday gift seasons. The nature of your book is a major consideration. Timing may be dictated by the nature of your book, the audience or industries you intend to reach.

Set a **publication date** far enough in the future to allow for time to print, submit for review, generate advance sales and take advantage of any timing features. Your publication date is not when your book comes back from the printer, but when it is released for sale to the audience.

How does your book fit with what's going on in the community, region or country? Trends influence people's opinions and behavior. Be prepared to take advantage of emerging trends and events which align with your book's message. See *Chase's Annual Events Directory* in the library.

> *"I skate where the puck is going to be,*
> *not where it has been."*
> *- Wayne Gretzky*

Who Can Help

Promoting a book requires skill in many areas. Writing and printing a book is only half the effort. The following resources will help author/publishers bring their book to the marketplace. Recognize your limitations. Seek a professional when one is needed.

❑ **Publicist.** A Publicist is a professional in the business of generating publicity for a company, individual or event. A publicist is the liaison between the author and the media. Most publishers agree that a new book needs publicity, but many find themselves unable to generate the type of reviews and media attention their book deserves. When using a publicist you are buying: contacts, inside information, industry advice for preparing and coaching you for media interviews and strategies based upon you and your book's strengths. Fees can range from $500 to more than $5000 a month. Although some publicists will work on a per placement basis (you pay only when you're scheduled), most work on a flat retainer fee. Ultimately the fee will be offset by the income generated from book sales. Find a publicist who *specializes* in books, and of course, check references. When your time is critical, hire a pro. Check the phone book under Publicists or Public Relations and contact your newspaper's book review editor and ask for a referral. The following website lists organizations who specialize in publicizing books:

www.absolute-sway.com/pfp/html/publicists.html

❏ **Associations.** The following trade associations represent author/publishers of books, audios, videos and CDs, providing numerous membership and cooperative promotional programs. Ask about their membership services:

National Association of Independent Publishers (NAIP)
Box 430
Highland City FL 33846
(863) 648-4420
www.publishersreport.com

Publishers Marketing Associations (PMA)
627 Aviation Way
Manhattan Beach CA 90266
(310) 372-2732
www.pma-online.org

Small Publishers Association of North America (SPAN)
Box 1306
Buena Vista CO 81211
(719) 395-4790
www.spannet.org

❏ **Continuing Education.** Educate yourself about the book trade. Keep abreast of the constant changes in the publishing industry. Learn about what is working and what doesn't. The following organization offers an array of seminars and workshops for the author/publisher:

Publishers University
Publishers Marketing Association
627 Aviation Way
Manhattan Beach CA 90266
(310) 372-2732
www.pma-online.org

❏ **Speaking Skills.** The ability to speak in front of groups is an essential skill for authors. The following organizations can help you gain the confidence and abilities to speak in public:

Dale Carnegie & Associates
1475 Franklin Avenue
Garden City NY 11530
(800) 231-5800
www.dalecarnegie.com

Toastmasters International
Box 9052
Mission Viejo CA 92690
(949) 858-1207
www.toastmasters.org

❏ **Book Marketing Newsletters.** Subscribe to a book marketing newsletter to keep current on industry trends, publicity tips and marketing ideas. Request a review copy and subscription rates.

Book Marketing Update
Bradley Communications Corp
135 E Plumstead Ave
Landsdowne PA 19050
(800) 784-4936
www.rtir.com

Book Marketing & Publicity
Infocom Group
5900 Hollis St Suite R2
Emeryville CA 94608
(800) 959-1059
www.infocomgroup.com

"A journey of a thousand miles begins with a single step."
- Chinese Proverb

❑   **Books to Read.** Benefit from other people's experiences by reading books on publishing and promotion. The following publications are worthwhile and referenced often. *These books can be ordered online at: www.wiseowlbooks.com/publish under Best Books.*

- **1001 Ways to Market Your Book** by John Kremer
  The most comprehensive book on marketing and promotion with strategies, resources, contacts and tips.

- **Publish to Win** by Jerrold R. Jenkins & Anne Stanton
  An easy to read book about selling through nontraditional markets.

- **Literary Market Place** by R.R. Bowker
  The industy's directory. This directory includes the names, addresses, phone numbers, and key contacts for thousands of book marketing channels and publicity outlets.

- **A Simple Guide to Self-Publishing** by Mark Ortman
  An instructive time and money saving handbook for preparing, printing, distributing and promoting your own book.

- **How to Market a Product for Under $500** by Jeffrey Dobkin
  A manual for marketing a product nationally on a modest budget using direct mail, advertising, news releases and the media to generate publicity and demand.

- **Words That Sell** by Richard Bayan
  A thesaurus of over 2500 words, prases and slogans to help write snappy and persuasive promotional copy for your flyers and ads.

"Besides using all the brains we have, we must use all we can borrow."

- Woodrow Wilson

What You Need to Promote a Book

There is no limit to what you can spend on promotional materials, so it becomes a question of budget and what is practical to convey your message. The following are common tools for the author/publisher and can be used in most promotional situations:

❏   **Media Kit.** A Media Kit (often termed Press Kit) simply provides more information about you and your book. This gives an editor, producer, reporter or interviewer useful information for a book review, interview or article.

The Media Kit includes:

- Cover Letter
- News Release
- An Author's Biography (written in the third person)
- Testimonial letters, news articles or endorsements
- Biography & Photo of the Author and the Book Cover
- Fact Sheet about the book
- Sample Interview Questions
- Brochure or Flyer
- Copy of your book or a book request postcard

Place the information in a glossy 8x11 pocket folder, or format and staple to fit inside an extra book cover. Both options provide an attractive and professional looking package. The key is for the information to be well organized and easy to read.

❏ **Cover Letter.** A cover letter is an introduction to the information that follows. Keep it brief, personable and professional. Cover letters are used in a variety of ways: to solicit reviews, seek distribution, introduce direct mail advertising and canvass for media interviews. In one or two paragraphs: summarize *what* you are offering, *why* it is unique or important and *how* people can benefit. Emphasize any special acknowledgments, recognitions, awards or events which shines favorable light on your message.

❏ **News Release (Press Release)** A news release is a one or two page (double spaced 200 words or less) write-up about your book or event. It is the most important, cost-effective publicity tool to a publisher. The closer your release is written to the accepted standard, the better its chance of being noticed. Write in the inverted pyramid style, with the most important information at the top, followed by more specific details below. Editors shorten a story from the bottom up. Make the release sound like news and avoid "the hype". Get to the point quickly. A news release is not advertising copy; it is designed to report information. Keep to the facts, leaving out flowery adjectives, superlatives and opinion. Emphasize throughout the release, the *Who, What, When, Where* and *Why* (or *How*) about the author, event or book. With so many books vying for publicity, what is it about you and your book that gives it news value (information which excites the editor)?

Your release should reflect the personality of your book by building around *one* central theme or news item. Separate news releases are used to announce an event, entice a media interview or spark a story. It's quite common to have a different release for each segment in your marketing plan. As often as possible, tie-in the release to a current event or trend. See a sample news release outline in the appendix on page 83.

News Releases need to answer three questions:
It is easy to read? Does it answer WHO, WHAT, WHEN,
WHERE and WHY? Do people need to know this information?

❏   **Reviews, Endorsements, Testimonials & Letters.** Save any reviews, endorsements, testimonials, fan mail and articles written about you or your book. These provide great sales copy for promotional literature and help support the credibility of the author and the book when soliciting publicity. The easiest way to get endorsements and testimonials is to ask for them. Seek experts, opinion leaders or celebrities in your field to review your manuscript (or finished book) and submit their impressions. Select endorsers who your audience may recognize. When soliciting endorsements, be sensitive to the many obligations of well known people and enclose a self-addressed stamped envelope for convenient return. Give acknowledgment to those who provide any manuscript reviews, editing or comments which land on the book cover. Send a complimentary autographed copy of your finished book to contributors and offer a wholesale discount to them on any future purchases. They may be interested in buying a small quantity for their friends and family. For endorsements, see *Contemporary Authors* at the library and search bookstores for books by other authors who have written on the same or similar subjects.

❏ **Articles.** Since you know more about your topic than most people, share your knowledge and promote your book at the same time. Most print media (newsletters, magazines, newspapers and journals) welcome newsworthy articles. Write a few carefully crafted, less than 500 word human interest or informational articles on yourself or the subject of your book. Write the article for the print media's audience. Because most news is planted, this is a common way of generating publicity. Some authors have even written an article which looks like a reporter's story and paid to have it placed as an advertisement in a newspaper or magazine with surprising results.

❏ **Photo.** Most interviewers want to know what you look like. Obtain 5x7 black & white promotional glossies of yourself and of the front cover of your book. Pictures are often requested by reviewers, magazines, newspapers and even bookstores to promote your signing. Have a photo which complements the message of your book. If you choose a professional photographer, make sure the photographer will let you make reprints. This will save you the cost of the photographer's markup. Label all photos with a sticker on the back with book title, author's name, publishing company and phone number.

❑ **Fact Sheet.** A fact sheet outlines the basic features or facts of your book. It includes: title, subtitle, description, author, ISBN number, book size, type of binding, page count, weight, number of books in a case, publication date, audience/market and wholesale availability. The fact sheet answers important questions for reviewers and the book trade. Include within your media kit.

❑ **Sample Interview Questions.** Make an interviewers job easier by having a question and answer sheet prepared in advance. Since you are the expert on the subject of your book, compile a list of interesting questions and short answers which make your book sound intriguing and appealing. This is a great way to practice your responses before doing media interviews.

❑ **Book Request Postcard.** A book request postcard allows the recipient to request a review copy of your book. Include one with your news release or media kit when you are not sending a review copy. Those interested in your message will respond, thus saving you the expense of mailing books to uninterested recipients.

❑ **Promotional Flyer or Postcard.** A full color 8-1/2x11 promotional flyer is enticing, professional and useful. Design your flyer to leave some blank space on which to photocopy a specific message at a future date. This enables you to adjust your flyer's message for many promotional situations. Match the design of your piece with the tone and market of your book. Is it humorous, professional, sporty or classy? Keep your message clear, succinct and benefit-oriented. The headline on top should grab people's attention so they want to read the rest. Remember that readers are interested in knowing what's in it for them. Consider offering a money back guarantee. These are comforting words for readers who rarely take advantage of a return. It reassures their purchasing decision. A 30 day guarantee is usually long enough, as most people ultimately will not follow through. Another popular option is a 4x6 color post card with your book's cover printed on one side and your message on the other. This is one way to reduce the postage and envelope costs when mailing. Compare, as print prices vary from printer to printer.

❑ **Extra Book Covers.** Extra book covers come in handy as mailers, point of purchase display or as part of the media kit. Many bookstores will request a book cover to help promote your event. Some distributors require extra covers for their sales force to use to present and sell your title. Order at least one hundred extra covers from the printer when your book goes to press.

❑ **Printed Stationery.** Ensure a professional business image with printed letterhead, envelopes, business cards and shipping labels with your name, address and logo. You want to instill confidence in people who may want to do business with you. The following companies offer discounted printed stationery.

Business Envelope Manufacturing Co
(800) 275-4400

The Stationery House
(800) 638-3033
www.stationeryhouse.com

❑ **Toll-Free 800/888 Number.** If a significant portion of your sales will be made direct to readers, set up your own toll-free 800/888 number. Most telephone carriers provide 800/888 service for a small monthly fee and a per minute usage charge. Choose a number that is easy to remember. Print this number on all of your promotional literature.

Contact the following about their service:

AT&T:	(800) 222-0400
MCI:	(800) 777-1099
Sprint:	(800) 366-1046

If not using your own toll-free number, consider using a fulfillment service *(page 40)* who will process incoming orders for you **or** list your distributor's number for order processing.

❏ **Credit Card & Check Acceptance.** Accepting credit cards and checks over the phone will make it easier for customers to purchase your book. Relying on people to mail a payment can result in lost or delayed sales. Despite their additional fees, credit card and checks-by-phone sales help your cash flow as the funds are credited to your bank account, usually within 24 hours. Establish a merchant credit-card account through PMA, SPAN *(page 18)* with your bank or by contacting:

Checks By Phone
301 E Yamoto Rd #2160
Boca Raton FL 33487
(561) 998-9020
www.checksbyphone.com

❏ **Voice Mail Service for the Telephone.** Avoid the clicking interruption announcing an incoming call, typical of call waiting. Voice mail activates when the line is busy allowing a caller to leave a message. This service is available, in most areas, through the local phone company at a reasonable monthly rate.

*95% of one's creative effort is spent
marketing one's creative effort.*

Alternative Promotional Materials

❑ **Galleys.** Often termed F&G (folded and gathered pages), a galley is not a finished book, but a bound representation of your finished book. This bound draft is mailed to pre-publication reviewers, months before the publication date, to announce a forthcoming book. Some reviewers require a book in this format before it even qualifies for a review. As an alternative to having galley proofs printed and bound, consider making copies of the camera-ready manuscript furnished to the printer. Use these as the galley. The following companies specialize in producing bound galleys.

Green Publications, Inc
23 Alabama Ave
Island Park NY 11558
(888) 259-4691
www.laserbooks.com

Crane Duplicating
947 Main St Rte 28
S Harwich MA 02661
(888) 940-1155
www.craneduplicating.com

❑ **Specialty Advertising.** If your budget permits, imprinted pens, bookmarks, T-shirts, buttons, coffee mugs and posters. They are fun giveaways and a reminder of your book. In fact, it is not uncommon to charge people for unique or unusual specialty advertising items. Request a catalog from the following company or see your local phone book under specialty advertising.

Best Impressions
Box 802
LaSalle IL 61301
(800) 635-2378
www.bestimpressions.com

❑ **Point of Purchase & Exhibit Displays.** Counter space is at a premium in retail stores. Displays (dumps) make visibility high using the least amount of space while drawing attention to the book. When conveniently placed near a cash register, for example, impulsive purchases can be encouraged. When seeking specialty retailers as a wholesale account, add value to quantity purchases by providing a display with each order. As reorders appear, use your success at one retail outlet to help you sell to another. The following companies sell point-of-purchase displays to publishers:

Clear Solutions
Box 2460
West Brattleboro VT 05303
(800) 257-4550
www.cleardisplays.com

Siegel Display Products
Box 95
Minneapolis MN 55440
(800) 626-0322
www.siegeldisplay.com

When exhibiting at trade shows and conventions, consider the appeal of a professional modular display. An attractive display can draw attention to your booth or table, thus encouraging traffic to stop and browse.

Godfrey Group
Box 90008
Raleigh NC 27675
(919) 544-6504
www.godfreygroup.com

Skyline Displays, Inc.
11901 Portland Ave S
Burnsville MN 55337
(800) 328-2725
www.skylinedisplays.com

❏ **Fax-on-Demand.** Fax-on-demand allows people to get information about you, your book or services 24 hours a day. This feature is initiated when callers phone from their fax machine and by following the voice prompts, they can order documents of information using their telephone keypad. The system retrieves the specified documents and prints them out on the caller's fax machine instantly. Publishers can purchase the equipment and software themselves or contract a fax-on-demand service listed below.

Infaxamation
1670 Broadway #2250
Denver CO 80202
(800) 329-4632
www.itgnet.com

❏ **900 Numbers.** This is a way to sell information on a pay-per-call basis. It is best suited to selling information, rather than selling a product. Beyond the initial setup and maintenance cost, advertising your 900 number will be the single greatest expense. 900 numbers work best if you have a low-cost advertising vehicle, such as a syndicated column in a national publication, where you can list your number at the end of the article. The following book will instruct you on how to set up a 900 number: *900 Know-How: How To Succeed With Your Own 900 Number Business* by Robert Maston and Carol Morse Ginsburg.

❏ **Press Clipping Service.** Few reviewers will send a tear sheet or copy of their review. If you are doing extensive publicity, a press clipping service will keep tabs on all articles, reviews, features or mentions that appear in print media. Contact the following companies about their services.

Bacon's Clipping Bureau
332 S Michigan Ave #900
Chicago IL 60604
(800) 621-0561
www.baconinfo.com

Competitive Edge
45 Wintonbury Ave
Bloomfield CT 06002
(888) 881-3343
www.clipresearch.com

"I am a publisher - a hybrid creature: one part stargazer, one part gambler, one part businessman and three parts optimist."

- Cass Canfield

Book promotion isn't about convincing people to buy your book. It's about knowing where to find the people who are waiting for it.

2. Book Distribution

How will people find your book if they want to buy it? Reviews, publicity and advertising are worthless unless your book is readily available to your audience. Your main objective is to place your title within easy access of the reader (distribution), **then** create a demand by letting people know about the book (promotion). The author/publisher must assume responsibility for creating the demand. There are actually two customers to consider: your distribution team and your audience. Marketing efforts must be allocated to both. At least 2-6 months before the release date, decide how you will distribute your book, whether through conventional, secondary or a combination of both channels. Establish a broad mix of distribution sites (barring an exclusive arrangement) to make your title readily available in places frequented by your audience.

> Make your distribution team an integral part of your promotional strategy by keeping them informed of your marketing plan.

• **Marketing Plan.** Most channels of distribution want to know how you are going to create the demand for your book before they decide to stock it. Prior to approaching any channel of distribution, have a detailed plan outlining *when, where* and *how* you are going to promote your book. Providing this will help selection committees justify their stocking decisions.

• **Consignments.** Books are sold on a consignment basis

unless negotiated otherwise. This means you don't get paid until after the book has been shipped from **their** warehouse. This is standard practice for the publishing industry, especially in the conventional channels of distribution. Books shipped to a wholesaler or distributor remain the property of the author/publisher until after a book has been ordered and shipped from their warehouse. They then pay 30-90 days later. All unsold books are returned to the publisher when the demand ceases, often at their own expense. A 15-25% return rate is common, so distributing your book in the wrong places, or a lack of promotion can only increase the return rate.

❏ **Discount Schedule and Policy.** Set a discount policy, in writing, from the very start. Make it simple and clear so there can be no misunderstanding. It is a requirement by the Federal Trade Commission (FTC) that discounts offered to any dealer must be provided to similar dealers buying the same quantity. Terms may differ when dealing with conventional channels of distribution since many work on a consignment basis. Create *separate* "terms and discounts" sheets for Wholesalers, Bookstores and Special Sales (Secondary channels of distribution) because standard discounts and terms will differ for each *(See sample on page 82)*. Include in your Terms and Conditions statement:

- Who pays the shipping and from what location
- Breakdown of the quantity discount schedule
- Payment terms
- How to establish credit with you
- Return policy (if any) and who pays what shipping
- Special services such as *dropshipping & S.T.O.P.s*

- **Shipping & Mailing Books.** When shipping pallets of books, use national trucking lines listed in the phone book. Their rates are based upon shipping location, weight and class of freight. Paperback books have a different and less expensive freight class than standard book rate class (class 60 and 65 respectively). UPS offers service for smaller quantities and will pickup and deliver for contracted customers. Single copies can be mailed most economically through the US Postal Service at *Book Rate*, or the slightly lower *Library Rate* when mailing to Libraries. The Post Office also offers *Priority Mail* for a bargain price as compared with the overnight express services, if delay by an extra day or two doesn't make a difference. The postal service will supply free priority envelopes, cardboard letter packs and mailing labels. Shipping expenses add up quickly, so managing postage and shipping costs is good business practice. If you are mailing large quantities on a regular basis, the phone book lists mailing services who specialize in sending bulk mass quantities.

Conventional Channels of Distribution

❑ **Bookstores.** There are many kinds: general, used, childrens, college, online and religious to list a few. Independently owned stores account for nearly half of all the bookstores in the United States. Bookstores purchase the majority of their books through wholesalers or distributors. Having your book stocked and displayed in bookstores is far more difficult and costly than having your book available through wholesalers. Most bookstores prefer buying through a wholesaler or distributor because they carry numerous titles which simplifies the bookstore's ordering procedure. Bookstores will special order unstocked books at a customer's request, reserving valuable shelf space for faster moving books. They typically purchase at a 40% discount off the list price. Selling books to bookstores is a three step process. First, establish a vendor account with a book wholesaler or distributor. Second, encourage the bookstore to purchase through your wholesaler or distributor. Finally, actively promote so people request to buy your book from bookstores. Bookstores and libraries rely heavily on mailed flyers to let them know what new books are available. Take advantage of this fact by sending a mailing to them at regular intervals, drawing attention to your title. *The American Book Trade Directory* by RR Bowker in the library has a complete listing of bookstores and wholesalers or contact the ABA listed below.

American Booksellers Association (ABA)
828 S Broadway
Tarrytown NY 10591
(800) 637-0037
www.bookweb.org

> Get into Bookstores through the *PMA Trade Distribution Program*. Twice a year a committee of representatives from major wholesale houses and chain bookstores convene to review all submitted titles (finished books only) and either accept or reject the proposed title. There is a small fee for this service. Call PMA at (310) 372-2732.

❏ **Chain Bookstores.** A rapidly growing segment of the industry is the chain and superstore, such as: Barnes & Noble and Borders Books & Music. Their inventories are tightly controlled with short shelf lives for slow-moving books. Recognize the risk of selling to the chains. They may order your entire stock, pay you 90 days later, leaving you to finance the next printing. Then, all of a sudden, they return the unsold books requesting a refund. Depending on your budget, a more cautious approach would be to coordinate purchases and promotional efforts with local or regional chain buyers. This way, the sales of one area will finance your expansion into another. Why risk putting all your books in one basket? When selling to the chains, let them know of your promotional plans and which wholesalers or distributor stock your title. This reduces their purchasing risk; knowing they can return books to a wholesaler or distributor rather than to a small publisher who may have left the business. When you call, specify the type of book (hard cover, trade paper) and genre, and ask for the buyer's name and request submission requirements. Being carried by the chains is an important link in your marketing campaign, especially for nationally promoted books. A strong showing in one chain could be the springboard to others. For larger promotional budgets, inquire about store merchandising programs for publishers to position books on counter and end displays.

Barnes & Noble
105 Fifth Ave
New York NY 10011
(212) 633-3377
www.barnesandnoble.com

Books-A-Million
402 Industrial Ln
Birmingham AL 35211
(205) 942-3737
www.booksamillion.com

Borders Books & Music
100 Phoenix Dr
Ann Arbor MI 48108
(734) 477-1100
www.borders.com

Chapters Books Canada
82 Peters St
Toronto ON M5V 2G5
(416) 263-5036
wwww.chapters.ca

❏ **Online Bookstores (Internet).** These are businesses with a Web Site on the Internet and who will list your title in their electronic bookstore. People around the world can browse a book's contents, read excerpts and get ordering information from their computer. There are several types of online bookstores, for instance: **Retail Sites** (Amazon Advantage and Book Sense) who sell books similar to a conventional bookstore, but by mail; **Referral Sites** (BookZone and ReadersNdex) where the publisher pays a small listing fee and retail orders are directed to the publisher for fulfillment and **Specialized Sites** who cater to niche or special interest markets. Many of these bookstores have services other than selling books: writing and publishing resources, online author interviews, chat rooms, directories, book reviews and other helpful information to attract people to their sites. Have your title listed in their online catalog by visiting the site and follow the prompts listed "Publishers" or phone directly. Usually, a listing with Ingram Book Company will get your book listed with the online bookstores. Be cautious about signing *any* exclusive agreement to your book's electronic rights.

Amazon Books
1200 12th Ave S
Seattle WA 98144
(206) 622-2335
www.amazon.com

Book Sense
Independent Booksellers Online
828 S Broadway
Tarrytown NY 10591
(800) 637-0037
www.booksense.com

The Bookzone
Box 9642
Scottsdale AZ 85252
(800) 536-6162
www.bookzone.com

ReadersNdex
Box 4786
Englewood CA 80155
(720) 253-5855
www.readersndex.com

❏ **Book Wholesalers.** Wholesalers stock, pick, pack, ship, collect, and then, pay you 90 days later on the orders received for your book. For this service, they want a 55% discount off the list price. Most are "Demand Wholesalers" meaning they fulfill orders for your book based upon the demand that you have created. In other words, wholesalers do not create the demand, they only satisfy it. When sales at the retail level are poor, returns are likely. Some publishers can have difficulty securing a wholesaler. If so, go out and create the demand for your book. If enough people ask for your book, the wholesaler will be forced to stock the title. There are hundreds of book wholesalers in the country, some national, some regional and many specializing in niche markets. Some wholesalers may help you develop a marketing plan hoping you include their advertising services as part of the plan. If a wholesale channel rejects your title, call and ask why. The rejection may be based on a negotiable point. To find wholesaler's specialties, consult the *American Book Trade Directory* and *Literary Market Place* in the library.

The shortest and best way to make a fortune in business is
to let other people see that it is in their interest to support yours.

• **Regional Book Wholesalers.** Is your book primarily of local or regional interest? Ask local booksellers through which regional wholesalers do they order. As a sound strategy for single title publishers, secure a vendor account with a regional wholesaler. Fan out as one area's sales supports the growth into another. Eventually, a strong case can be made to step up to national wholesalers. See a list of wholesalers in the appendix on page 87.

• **National Book Wholesalers.** Ingram Book Company and Baker & Taylor Books are the nation's largest general book wholesalers with branches throughout the United States. Contact both of them, with a complete marketing plan, and inquire as to how to start a vendor account.

Baker & Taylor Books	**Ingram Book Company**
1120 Rte 22 E	One Ingram Blvd
Bridgewater NJ 08807	LaVergne TN 37086
(908) 541-7476	(800) 937-8100
www.btol.com	www.ingrambook.com

❏ **Book Distributors.** Book distributors differ from book wholesalers (although the words are used synonymously) in that they sell your book through commissioned sales representatives and a catalog. Depending on your book, a master distributor can introduce your title to wholesalers and bookstores for you, thus freeing you to concentrate on promotional efforts. Distributors typically buy at a 55% to 65% discount off the list price (plus inbound shipping). Some may require an exclusive arrangement. Before signing an exclusive agreement, clarify what is meant by "exclusive". Do not limit your book to an exclusive arrangement that prevents you from selling to markets to which the distributor does not sell. Some exclusive agreement clauses are negotiable and subject to revision. Contact distributors 2-6 months prior to your book's release, allowing enough time to go through their selection process. See the *Literary Market Place* or the *American Book Trade Directory* in the library for complete listings. The following pages define the various types of distributors.

• **Independent Distributors.** Also known as IDs or Jobbers, distribute mass market paperbacks, magazines and some regional or local titles. If your book fits their format, they will place your title in non-bookstore locations such as drugstores, supermarkets, department stores, airports, military bases and newsstands. Their discount is 55% off list price. IDs traditionally have a high return rate and a short shelf life. If a book doesn't sell fast, it is replaced. Require all returns in resalable condition since most IDs will return just the cover (stripped) asking for full credit.

• **Specialty Distributors.** If your book is targeted toward a specific market niche or subject area (outdoor, health, ethnic, christian, food etc.), specialty distributors can help you reach those readers. Their discounts are between 55% to 65% off the list price and most work on a nonexclusive basis. Specialty distributors welcome the submission of quality books with strong marketing plans that fit their genre. See the *Literary Market Place* or the *American Book Trade Directory* in the library for a complete listing.

• **National Library Distributors.** There are more than 100,000 libraries in the United States ranging from Academic to Public, and they purchase about 14% of all the books published. Libraries purchase copies for circulation and then your title becomes a permanent advertisement while sitting on their shelves. If patrons find value in your book, they may decide to buy a copy for their personal use. Most libraries purchase through wholesalers or one of the library distributors listed below. Contact these two distributors and ask for a vendor application. Both work on consignment requiring a 55% discount and pay 90 days later.

Quality Books
1003 W Pines Rd
Oregon IL 61061
(815) 732-4450
www.quality-books.com

Unique Books
5010 Kemper Ave
St Louis MO 63139
(314) 776-6695

• **Master Distributors.** If your book is of general interest and you plan to promote your title nationally, consider a master distributor to carry your title. A master distributor will get your book to the regional and national wholesalers, and perhaps present your title to major independent and chain bookstores. They will coordinate your promotional efforts with their sales network. These distributors want a 65% discount off the list price, plus monthly fees. Most will want an exclusive right to sell to the book trade which leaves you to sell through the secondary channels. Most master distributors prefer publishers with more than one title. However, a strong marketing plan, a promotion-oriented author and a well designed book may influence a single title decision. If they reject your title, ask why and who they might recommend. Choose an exclusive distributor carefully to insure a proper fit between your title and it's market. If you decide to use an exclusive distributor, call three of their publisher-clients for references before committing yourself. Request the title acquisition procedure from the following master distributors:

BookWorld Services, Inc.
1933 Whitfield Park Loop
Sarasota FL 34243
(941) 758-8094
www.bookworld.com

Login Publishers Consortium
1436 W Randolph St
Chicago IL 60607
(312) 432-7650
www.lb.com

ACCESS Publishers Network
6893 Sullivan Rd
Grawn MI 49637
(616) 276-5196
www.accesspublishers.com

Associated Publishers Group
1501 County Hospital Rd
Nashville TN 37218
(615) 254-2450
www.apgbooks.com

Independent Publishers Group
814 N Franklin St
Chicago IL 60610
(312) 337-0747
www.ipgbook.com

National Book Network
4720 Boston Way
Lanham MD 20706
(800) 462-6420
www.nbnbooks.com

Publishers Group West
1700 4th St
Berkeley CA 94710
(510) 528-1444
www.pgw.com

Consortium Book Distribution
1045 Westgate DR
St Paul MN 55114
(651) 221-9035
www.cbsd.com/books

❏ **Publishers Who Distribute.** In addition to their own books, some publishers also distribute titles from other publishers, expanding their product line. Contact publishers where there is market fit and inquire about submission requirements. See the *LMP.*

❏ **Independent Sales Representatives.** When deciding to manage your own distribution, solicit the help of commissioned sales reps to make sales calls within the trade. However, most reps prefer to work with publishers who release many new titles a year, so this may not be an option for the self-publisher. Typically, reps carry several publishers' lines and hand sell books to bookstores and wholesalers. They insist on protected or exclusive territories, earning a commission on any sale in their territory. Their commission is usually 5-10% above the standard book trade discounts. Contact NAIPR for a directory and guideline for publishers.

National Association of Independent Publishers Representatives (NAIPR)
111 East 14th St PMB 157
New Yok NY 10003
(888) 624-7779
www.naipr.org

❏ **Fulfillment Services.** These companies offer warehousing and order-processing services (toll-free numbers & credit card purchases over the phone) for your book. Most want a 50% discount or smaller percentage plus monthly service fees. As you promote your title, make reference to your service's 800 number for ordering 24 hours a day. Contact the following about their programs:

Publication Services, Inc
8803 Tara Ln
Austin TX 78737
(512) 288-5021
www.psifulfillment.com

Upper Access
Box 457
Hinesburg VT 05461
(800) 310-8320
www.upperaccess.com

BookMasters, Inc.
2541 Ashland Rd
Mansfield OH 44905
(419) 589-5100
www.bookmasters.com

The Intrepid Group, Inc
1331 Red Cedar Cr
Fort Collins CO 80524
(970) 493-3793
www.intrepidgroup.com

Secondary & Special Channels of Distribution

Some books do not have broad based, general appeal for conventional channels of distribution. Special interest or niche books may find secondary channels the easiest to secure and, the most profitable. Most books are sold in the United States through secondary or special markets. So independent publishers must plan to produce more of their sales from secondary, rather than conventional markets. Read the report: *Increased Availability of Books Through Non-Traditional Retailers* by contacting BISG, a nonprofit industry study group listed below. Consult the *Literary Market Place* for additional listings of secondary and special channel contacts.

Book Industry Study Group (BISG)
160 Fifth Ave
New York NY 10010
(212) 929-1393
www.bisg.org

❏ **Catalog Houses.** Have you ever received a catalog in the mail that featured books? Thousands of companies in the United States send out catalogs annually, many including books, and some dedicated solely to books. Catalogs redefine specialization as there are catalogs available for nearly every market niche imaginable. Find the companies with the right product lines and image fit. Then send them a persuasive cover letter with a review copy for each book you are submitting. Be clear on your discount terms, yet willing to negotiate. Catalogs have an extremely long lead time, so plan well in advance for submission. Most catalog companies pay after 30 days and want a 40-60% discount. For mail order catalogs that feature books, see *Directory of Mail Order Catalogs,* the *National Directory of Catalogs* and *Literary Market Place* at the public library. Search online through (www.buyersindex.com) with over 5000 mail order catalog companies indexed.

❏ **Book Subsidiary Rights.** This is when you sell the rights to all or a portion of your book to someone who will repackage or reproduce it in a different format. Some rights include: Book Clubs, Movie/TV, Serial/Excerpt (newspaper/magazine reprint), Foreign (translation) Paperback or Hardcover, Electronic, Dramatic and Merchandising. Consider hiring an agent or attorney familiar with the right you are selling so they can negotiate more effectively on your behalf. An agent's value lies in his network of relationships and areas of specialty. Any book subsidiary contract you sign must be strong, specific and protective.

• **Book Club Rights.** Book clubs may be interested in purchasing the rights to, or actual copies of your finished book. While some special interest book clubs will buy books regardless of the publication date, most prefer 6 to 9 months notice before the release date. If they are interested, some may offer an advance against royalties. Others may purchase copies at a deep discount. This is a way to offset your initial printing expenses. Book club sales build credibility for your book as their endorsement can be highlighted on the cover and other promotional literature. Listed below are the two largest book clubs who prefer to see your book early in galley or manuscript form. Inquire about their submission procedures. See *Literary Market Place* in the library which lists over 150 book clubs covering nearly every genre.

Book Span	Literary Guild of America
Time-Life Building	Bantam Doubleday Dell
1271 Avenue of the Americas	1540 Broadway
New York NY 10020	New York NY 10036
(212) 522-4200	(212) 782-7253
www.bookspan.com	www.booksonline.com

• **Serial & Excerpt Rights.** Some books are excellent candidates for serial reprint rights to magazines, newspapers and journals. Not only do reprint rights provide income, but valuable publicity for the book as well. Identify those publications most likely to be interested in your book's message and send a query letter 3-6 months before the release date. The sale of reprint rights to print media has two forms: first and second serial rights. First serial rights apply to forthcoming books and are sold prior to the publication date. Second serial rights are sold after the publication date. When an agreement is struck, get it in writing. If possible, negotiate nonexclusive first serial rights allowing you to sell different passages of the book to other periodicals. Exclusive rights should yield a higher rights fee. See *Literary Market Place* and *Standard Directory of Periodicals* in library for listings.

• **Foreign Rights.** You can expand your market by selling your book overseas. Author/publishers can sell translation rights to a foreign publisher or license reprints of the English version. Another option is to license or sell your book directly to an overseas distributor. Typically, technical, scientific, business and fiction titles sell best. Reach the overseas market by seeking an export agent to represent your title. Or contact the foreign distributors and publishers directly or display your title at an International Trade Show such as the Frankfurt or London Book Fairs *(see page 67)*. Trading internationally is not without risk. In addition to currency and credit risks, there is the very real issue of piracy. Protect your interests by seeking professional advice when venturing overseas. See the *Literary Market Place*.

❏ **Premium & Incentive.** Many businesses offer premium gift items as incentives to their employees and customers. Why couldn't that premium be your book? Book premiums are favorites among corporations. They make impressive gifts or are added value for customers who purchase their products. Find a good match between your book and a company philosophy or product line. With self-help or how-to books, printing a summary booklet as a premium may lead to actual book sales to readers. Companies usually want a 50-70% discount and pay in 30 days. Large quantity sales may choose manufacturing cost plus 10% with special cover changes imprinting that company's name and logo.

The Thomas Register of American Manufacturers has a web site with a massive directory of corporations and manufacturers around the country (www.thomasregister.com) or see their directory in the library. Also in the library: *Brands And Their Companies, A Gale Trade Names Directory* and the *Directory of Premium, Incentive & Travel Buyers.* Request a free information packet from IMRA.

Incentive Manufacturers Representatives Association (IMRA)
1805 N Mill St # A
Naperville IL 60563
(630) 369-3466
www.info-now.com/imra

❏ **Specialty Retail Outlets.** Not everyone buys books in bookstores. There are tens of thousands of alternative outlets for books in the United States. They can include: home improvement centers, drugstores, auto supply dealers, gourmet shops, health food stores, museums and health clubs, to list a few. Approach retail outlets who can tie your book sales to their product merchandising. Show them your book can be an added profit, especially if they are unaccustomed to carrying books. Your book will not compete with as many titles as in a bookstore. After identifying the stores who may be interested, research and find out how their market works. Ask local store owners how they learn about and choose to carry products. Perhaps they can recommend a distributor or sales organization for you to contact. Most direct sales are made on a nonreturnable basis at a 40-50% discount.

❏ **Gift Stores.** More than 30% of the US population has never been in a bookstore. With some 150,000 specialty gift stores nation wide, having your book displayed in such retail outlets is a good way to reach those individual. Unlike bookstores, the gift market does not return books. However, the discount is higher; generally 50% off list price. If using gift representatives to present your title to buyers, expect another 10-15% commission above the standard discount, leaving you responsible for the shipping and invoicing of the books they sell. Many large cities have wholesale gift-center showrooms where companies and gift rep organizations display their wares for buyers to browse. Check the phone book for listings.

❑ **Mutual Interest Alliance.** There may be a link between your book and businesses, organizations or individuals who regularly serve customers interested in the subject of your book. Enlist the marketing efforts of others who want to make money selling your products along side their own. Perhaps you can cross-promote, selling their product as well. Authors who speak to groups typically sell their own and others' books during their lecture or workshop. Why couldn't one of those books be yours? Offer your book at a 40-50% discount, depending upon quantity purchased.

❑ **Warehouse Clubs & Discount Stores.** Warehouse clubs and discount stores now account for over 10% of all book sales. This is another way to reach people who may not shop at conventional bookstores. While their book selection may be narrow, they purchase large quantities at one time. This can be risky for a one or two book publisher. Whereas offering to test market in regional stores is often a safer option. Most prefer to purchase through book wholesalers or distributors. If your book has a seasonal or holiday theme, make it available well in advance of that occasion. Contact the book buyers at the following warehouse clubs and discount stores or inquire about a vendor account with AMS, as they specialize in selling direct to warehouse clubs:

Advance Marketing Services
5880 Oberlin Dr #400
San Diego CA 92121
(858) 457-2500
www.admsweb.com

K-Mart Stores
3100 W Big Beaver Rd
Troy MI 48084
(248) 643-1000
www.bluelight.com

Sam's Wholesale Club
608 SW 8th St
Bentonville AR 72712
(501) 277-7546
www.samsclub.com

Price/Costco
999 Lake Dr
Issaquah WA 98027
(425) 313-8100
www.costco.com

Target Stores
Box 1392
Minneapolis MN 55440
(612) 304-6073 x6365
www.target.com

❏ **TV Shopping Networks.** TV shopping networks reach more than 50 million households in the United States providing the convenience of shopping from home. Books are becoming a growing part of the Networks' product mix, selling thousands of copies in a short period of time. Send your book to the vendor relations department for consideration. Call beforehand to confirm the submission requirements. They usually purchase at a 50% discount, buying on consignment (with return privileges).

Home Shopping Network
Box 9090
Clearwater FL 34618
(727) 872-1000
www.hsn.com

QVC
1365 Enterprise Dr
West Chester PA 19380
(610) 701-8282
www.qvc.com

❏ **Associations.** There are more than 18,000 trade, professional and special interest associations in the United States, providing a convenient way to reach a tightly targeted audience. Contact associations where your book supports their mission and philosophy. When an association agrees to carry your book, there is an implied endorsement. Most associations require a 50% discount or less. Inquire about their resource catalog (which usually includes books) mailed to their members. Some associations will rent their membership mailing lists to nonmembers. Ask about the date and location of their annual convention. In the library, see the *Encyclopedia of Associations* by the Gale Group.

❏ **Fund Raiser.** Most nonprofit organizations such as churches, civic groups, or schools are looking for ways to raise money. When there is a subject fit, donate a percentage of your sales to their cause in exchange for selling and endorsing your book. Offer a quantity discount of 40-50% negotiating returns.

❏ **Academic Market.** Within this vast arena, this book will focus on the sale of trade books instead of textbooks, which could be a volume unto itself. Selling in the academic market requires an applicable book and lots of effort. The three major purchasers of trade books: college bookstores, school libraries and teacher supply stores, will buy direct from publishers, wholesalers and distributors. Tradebooks which appeal to students, or become suggested reading by an instructor, can fare well in college bookstores and libraries. Mailing lists of teacher-supply stores are readily available from list brokers. Reviews, direct mailing and exhibitions at academic conventions are three common ways to promote within this market. Follett runs the largest chain of college bookstores. NACS is an academic trade association with many programs for publishers. See *Literary Market Place* in the library for a complete listing of academic distributors.

Follett College Stores
2233 West St
River Grove IL 60171
(800) 621-4345
www.follett.com

National Association of College Stores
500 E Lorain St
Oberlin OH 44074
(800) 622-7498
www.nacs.org

❏ **Government Markets.** The United States Government is the world's largest purchaser of goods and service, and they buy books. The Small Business Administration (www.sba.gov) has a mandate to ensure small businesses receive a certain percentage of government purchases. Because of this, most government agencies have programs assisting the small business owner. Marketing to the government is not much different than marketing to any large organization. To get started, *The Federal Marketplace* (www.fedmarket.com) assists companies in marketing products to the federal government.

*"Publishing is a very mysterious business.
It is hard to predict what kind of sale
or reception a book will have."*

- Thomas Wolfe

3. Publicity
(Book Reviews & Media Interviews)

Publicity is essential to a book's success. Third party endorsements, such as favorable reviews and media appearances, yield much more credibility than can be purchased with advertising. The sheer volume of books released each year, and the limited print and air space available, makes for fierce competition for these resources.

To think publicity is free is a misnomer considering the costs of review copies, media kits, postage and the author's travel expenses. However, it is still the least expensive way to promote your book. Publicity can sell books for far less money than paid advertising, while it generates credibility, interest and a demand for your book. Yet, it is no guarantee that your book will sell. No one can predict the commercial success of a book. You can only give your book the best possible chance to succeed with the least amount of risk; then wait for the market to send its verdict.

- **Word-of-Mouth Advertising.** Word-of-mouth can be the fastest and most efficient form of publicity. This happens when people have heard, seen, bought or read your book and then told others about it. Anything you can do to get people talking about your book will generate interest and sales. Each purchase becomes a potential word-of-mouth referral for another. Create a buzz. In the book trade this means people are talking about your book. An enthusiastic recommendation does wonders to motivate a friend or colleague to buy. Reviews, interviews, giveaways to opinion leaders and even paid advertising, all contribute to word-of-mouth exposure. The more books in people's hands, the greater the likelihood they will spread the word. With the Internet, this occurs even more quickly. Success begets success.

Pre-Publication Reviews

Besides yourself, who could think your book is great? Pre-publication reviews are directed at the trade (libraries, wholesalers and bookstores) **before** the publication date and the release of your book. This helps the trade evaluate new titles, and influences its purchasing decisions.

❏ **Trade Reviews.** To be reviewed, at least **90** days *before* the publication date, the major trade review magazines want to see: a galley (NOT a finished book), a fact sheet, author's bio, any endorsements from respected authorities, publicity plans, wholesale availability and a *brief* cover letter stating *what* the book is about, *why* you wrote it and *how* it is unique from others on the market. Send all of this by first class mail. This is no guarantee your book will be reviewed. However, even one favorable review could generate substantial advance sales. In addition, any reviews you receive can be used on your promotional literature and printed on the back cover of reprinted books. It is worth a phone call to inquire about the full name (with correct spelling) of the person to whom you will submit a review package along with any special submission guidelines. Follow-up all submissions with a finished book. See *Literary Market Place* in the library for additional review sources.

Booklist
American Library Assn
50 E Huron St
Chicago IL 60611
(312) 944-6780
www.ala.org

Chicago Tribune Books
435 N Michigan Ave
Chicago Il 60611
(312) 222-3232
www.chicagotribune.com

Kirkus Reviews
200 Park Ave S
New York NY 10003
(212) 777-4554
www.kirkus.com

L.A. Times Book Review
Times Mirror Square
Los Angeles CA 90053
(213) 237-5000
www.latimes.com

N.Y. Times Book Review
229 W 43rd St
New York NY 10036
(212) 556-1234
www.nytimes.com

San Francisco Chronicle Book Review
901 Mission St
San Francisco CA 94103
(415) 777-7042
www.sfgate.com

Bloomsbury Review
1553 Platte St #206
Denver CO 80202
(303) 455-3123
www.bookforum.com/bloomsbury

Library Talk
480 E Wilson Bridge Rd #L
Worthington OH 43085
(614) 436-7107
www.linworth.com

Library Journal
245 W 17th St
New York NY 10011
(212) 463-6818
www.libraryjournal.com

N.Y. Review of Book
1755 Broadway
New York NY 10019
(212) 757-8070
www.nybooks.com

Publishers Weekly
245 W 17th St
New York NY 10011
(212) 463-6758
www.publishersweekly.com

Independent Publisher Online
121 E Front St 4th Fl
Traverse City MI 49684
(616) 933-0445
www.bookpublishing.com

School Library Journal
245 W 17th St
New York NY 10011
(212) 463-6759
www.slj.com

Post-Publication Reviews

Post-publication reviews from the print media are intended to reach your potential reader. Book reviews are one of the most cost-effective methods for promoting your book. It is very expensive and inefficient to send review copies to every review source. Thus, before your publication date, research and compile a list of those review sources which will provide the best opportunity for a review.

Search for general and specialized newsletters, magazines, journals, experts in the field, associations and any organization that would find interest in the subject of your book. When you get a great review, use it! Send a copy to your wholesalers, add it to your advertising and include an excerpt on the cover of your next reprint. Beware, some reviewers will review any book for a fee, thus diminishing the credibility of the review. If paying for an ad is *not* contingent upon printing your review, consider placing a small advertisement in the reviewed issue. Double your exposure by advertising in the issue following your review.

Submitting review copies may not yield a review for weeks to several months and sometimes more than a year later. Upon receipt of your books from the printer, mail review copies immediately to your compiled review sources.

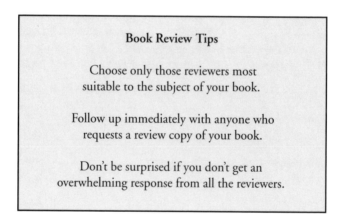

Book Review Tips

Choose only those reviewers most
suitable to the subject of your book.

Follow up immediately with anyone who
requests a review copy of your book.

Don't be surprised if you don't get an
overwhelming response from all the reviewers.

Giving books away can become an expensive proposition, particularly when you include the cost of postage. Generally, budget at least 5 to 10% of the books from your first printing for review copies and give them to people who can do you the most good. Despite the expense, giveaways are an essential investment when compared to the cost of other forms of promotion. Stamp REVIEW COPY on any copy you give away to discourage people from selling or returning that book to a wholesaler for a refund. Keep good records, as giveaways are a tax deductible expense.

❏ **Newspapers.** Newspaper book reviewers receive more solicitations each day than they can review in a month. Review space is at a premium. Nevertheless, any mention of your book will help sales. If your book has a wide general appeal, mail a news release and book request postcard (or book) to the major daily newspapers, targeting the appropriate editor (Features, Business, Food, etc.). Ideally, mail before the publication date or as soon as your books are received from the printer. Local newspapers and magazines are your best sources for a review or an news article. Remember, a newspaper is a community servant. Because you are local news, they will be more inclined to give you preference over others. You may want to rent a mailing list to reach newspapers. *See page 75-76.*

❏ **News Wire Service.** Send a news release to the news wire services listed below. If your message has important news value, they may send your release (edited or unedited) to hundreds of wire service subscribers around the country. Begin by submitting a news release to the local or regional offices listed in the phone book, and one to the main office listed below. Call to inquire about the name of the appropriate editor. If the story is truly time-sensitive, send a news release via fax and follow up with a phone call later the same day. Additional news syndications can be found in *Gebbie's All in One Directory* at the library.

Associated Press (AP)
50 Rockefeller Plaza
New York NY 10020
(212) 621-1500
www.ap.org

Dow Jones
Plaza Two
34 Exchange Pl
Jersey City NJ   07311
(201) 938-4370
www.dowjones.com

Reuters America, Inc
199 Water St
New York NY 10038
(212) 859-1600
www.reuters.com

United Press International (UPI)
11 Penn Plaza #937
New York NY 10001
(212) 564-5901
www.upi.com

Good luck has the scent of perspiration around it.

❏ **Magazines.** Research magazines where subscribers' interests match the subject of your book. Find out what magazines your audience reads and send a copy of your book and a press release (or media kit) to their book review editors. Some magazines devote an issue to a special focus. Inquire about their upcoming subject focus. See the *Standard Periodical Directory* in the library for listings of specialty magazines.

❏ **Newsletters.** The number of newsletters has boomed during the past decade, now accounting for nearly one-third of all publications. This has resulted in more opportunities to get your book mentioned or reviewed. In addition to independent newsletters, most associations publish a newsletter which is mailed to their members and often has a book review section. Some large foundations and associations with newsletters may even be interested in sponsoring your book to their members for a share of the profit. See the *Directory of Newsletters* and *Encyclopedia of Associations* in the library.

❏ **Free Lance Reviewers.** Compile or rent a mailing list of free lance book reviewers around the country. Most of these reviewers have syndicated columns where their reviews will appear in several newspapers and magazines. Send a news release, fact sheet and a book request return postcard (or book) when you receive finished books from the printer. See *Literary Market Place* in the library.

❏ **Experts in the Field.** Send a review copy to opinion leaders, other authors and experts on the subject of your book, asking for their comments and endorsements. This is a wonderful way to get influential people talking about your book, lending to word-of-mouth advertising. See *Contemporary Authors* by Gale Group at the library.

"The critic is the only independent source of information. The rest is advertising."
- Pauline Kael

❑ **Book Awards & Contests.** Being nominated for an award can be a profitable and satisfying experience, generating publicity for your book. Some awards even carry cash prizes or money to finance a reprint. Any award you receive can be mentioned on your promotional material. Some publishers will place a sticker on the cover of the book to call attention to the nomination. Listed below are a few prestigious national awards. Phone for an application and submission requirements. See the *Literary Market Place* or *Writer's Market* in the library for a complete list of contests covering numerous special interest and subject categories.

The Pulitzer Prize Board
Columbia University
709 Journalism Bldg
New York NY 10027
(212) 854-3841
www.pulitzer.org

Ben Franklin Book Award
Publishers Marketing Association
627 Aviation Way
Manhattan Beach CA 90266
(310) 372-2732
www.pma-online.org

Writer's Digest Self-Published Book Award
F&W Publishing
1507 Dana Ave
Cincinnati OH 45207
(513) 531-2222
www.fwpublications.com

National Book Award
National Book Foundation
260 Fifth Ave #904
New York NY 10001
(212) 685-0261
www.nationalbook.org

Media Interviews

Print and electronic media (magazines, newspapers, television and radio) are under constant pressure to fill space or time with news. Media exposure gives an author expert status and provides legitimacy that even the largest advertising budget can't touch. However, not every book is appropriate for TV, radio or newsprint. Some books are too narrowly focused. Topics with a broad appeal fare much better. Practically every media source relies on unsolicited material about people, events and trends to fill its space or time. The media needs you as much as you need them. Unsolicited news releases occupy nearly 20% of editorial space.

The media is interested in attracting and keeping readers, listeners and viewers. Their revenues from advertising are dependent on this. Editors and producers are not interested in providing free advertising and publicity to publishers or authors. They are primarily concerned with providing information, news and entertainment that wins a larger audience. To get an interview, you must convince the editor or producer that your message will be of interest to the audience. A personable, photogenic, articulate or newsworthy author can fare well in this forum. On the local front, you and your book are news and should have an edge to get print space or air time.

Media interviews can be an unnerving experience for the novice. So, practice your message on smaller stations until your comfort and skill level rises. Authors must be able to sustain a full hour of conversation. Practice short answers then elaborate on them as needed to give you flexibility in shorter interview segments. Keep the language simple and define any terms that may not be familiar to the audience. People will buy your book if they feel connected to you or your message. Prepare anecdotes or personal stories, weaving examples with statistics which leave the listener or viewer yearning for more. Drop the name of the book in the conversation a couple of times. When mentioning your toll-free number, give listeners an incentive to order now by offering autographed copies, specialty gift items or free reports with their purchases.

> Handle an offbeat or hostile question during an interview with a bridging technique. Respond by saying: "I'm not an expert on that subject, but I can tell you about...".
> Then deliver the message you want.

Make it easier to interview you by providing the interviewer a list of questions and useful excerpts or statistics from your book to help guide the conversation. Think in sound bites. Prepare a 30 second explanation of your book and why it's important. Be alert and enthusiastic, and most importantly, be yourself. Follow-up each interview with a hand-written thank you note to the host or producer. Offer to fill in if another guest should suddenly cancel. See *The Directory of Publications and Broadcast Media* in the library for media listings.

The following companies sell ways to reach the national media:

Radio-TV Interview Report
Bradley Communications Corp.
135 E Plumstead Ave
Lansdowne PA 19050
(800) 989-1400
www.rtir.com

Talk Show Selects
Broadcast Interview Source
2233 Wisconsin Ave NW #301
Washington DC 20007
(800) 932-7266
www.yearbook.com

Parrot Media Network (www.parrotmedia.com) is a subscription based online resource directory of names, format and phone numbers of cable, TV, radio stations and newspapers in the United States.

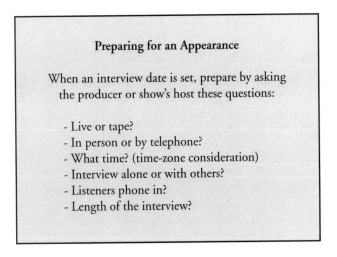

Preparing for an Appearance

When an interview date is set, prepare by asking the producer or show's host these questions:

- Live or tape?
- In person or by telephone?
- What time? (time-zone consideration)
- Interview alone or with others?
- Listeners phone in?
- Length of the interview?

"The oldest books are still only just out to those who have not read them."

- Samuel Butler

• **Radio.** Radio is your most accessible medium. If you enjoy talking about your book, you will enjoy radio interviews. There are more than 750 radio talk shows in the country looking for interesting guests. Many conduct interviews over the phone. Some will even tape an interview for airing at a future date. Radio stations are built around a central format such as newstalk, sports, entertainment, business or public affairs. Before you call, understand the format and demographics of the show, and gear your pitch to its audience.

When approaching stations for interviews, make sure you and your book's message sound interesting, entertaining or newsworthy. You must convince the program director that your message will hold an audience and that you can give an engaging interview. Program directors want shows that will make their audience feel something (laugh, cry, disagree or get angry). Phone and say: "I have a story that may be of interest to your audience". Be prepared to quickly explain why your message will be important to their listeners. Be creative in your pitch by perhaps presenting an actual idea for the show. Suggest a contest, quiz or giveaway to accompany your interview. Be mindful that you are selling a message, not a book. Mention the success on other radio shows to lend support to your interview experience. If the interview goes well, offer to be a last minute stand-in if a future guest cancels. The more stations you contact, the more interviews you will get. If your topic isn't time sensitive, schedule four to six weeks in advance.

Disable your call waiting feature before telephone interviews to avoid that annoying clicking interruption from incoming calls.

Let bookstores in the broadcast area know of any media appearances as they are likely to stock your book.

Avoid paying for interviews. Only stations with typically low ratings and under supported by advertisers will charge.

Start off by interviewing on smaller stations to practice your delivery for the larger ones. Assume interviewers have not read your book, as this is the case more often than not. Interviewers rely on the information in the media kit you sent them in advance.

• **Television.** Wouldn't it be ideal if the major national talk show hosts invited you to discuss your book on their show? TV leaves a powerful impression in viewers' minds and can translate into an explosion in book sales. When getting started, it is a more realistic goal to be a guest on the local afternoon news program or TV magazine talk show. Contact a show's producers with your message convincing them to interview you. Remember, a television appearance is not much different than radio, except sight has been added to sound. Dress appropriately to avoid detracting from the message you are delivering. National TV talk show producers may want to see a video of you on camera before an invitation is sent. Local cable access stations offer a great place to practice live interviews.

> When doing a live media interview, offer to leave a few books behind for prizes, giving you additional exposure as they promote the giveaways.

• **Newspapers.** More than 700 daily and weekly newspapers throughout the country are searching for news. Perhaps your book can address lifestyle, business, gardening, travel or cooking issues. How can you get your story in print? Send a news release and a cover letter about a possible story angle to the appropriate editor. If your book is about a topic that just hit the headlines, get on the phone and try to secure an interview. If interested, they will print the material you have sent or decide to send a reporter to cover the story. Op-Ed (Opposite-Editorial) pages of a newspaper offer another place for you to generate interest or controversy on the subject of your book. Newspapers offer guest columns or commentaries on a variety of subjects. In some cases, an accepted 600 to 800 word essay can earn the author a small fee.

- **Magazines.** Thousands of magazines cater to every audience you can imagine. Nearly every niche has a publication, trade association, journal or newsletter. Offer reprints of portions of your book in exchange for free advertising or a byline for the end of your article. Do not neglect local and regional publications as they may be more accommodating to the local author. See the *Standard Directory of Periodicals* and *The Encyclopedia of Associations* at the public library for a compete listing of national magazines and trade associations.

Getting Your Book Listed

Let the book trade know that you have published a book. Orders can come about most unexpectedly from having your title listed in several directories. Most of these listings are free. Make it easy for readers to find you and your book. Phone to request an application from the following:

International Standard Book Numbering Agency (ISBN)
When you submitted your **ABI** (Advanced Book Information) form with your publication date and ISBN number, you automatically get a listing in *Books in Print*.

Library of Congress Catalog Card Number.
When you requested your LC number, your book was listed in a catalog enabling libraries to locate your book more easily.

Cumulative Book Index & Vertical File Index
H.W. Wilson Co
950 University Ave
Bronx NY 10452
(718) 588-8400
www.hwwilson.com

Small Press Record of Books in Print &
International Directory of Little Magazines and Small Presses.
Dustbooks
Box 100
Paradise CA 95967
(916) 877-6110
www.dustbooks.com

ABA Book Buyers Handbook
American Bookseller Association
828 S Broadway
Tarrytown NY 10591
(800) 637-0037
www.bookweb.org

Publishers Directory and Contemporary Authors
Gale Group
27500 Drake Rd
Farmington Hills MI 48331
(800) 347-4253
www.galegroup.com

❏ **Getting Mentioned in Other Books and Directories.** Would your book serve as a good reference? Have your book listed as a resource in the appendix or bibliography of other people's work. Visit bookstores and libraries to review books including information about the subject of your own book. Write down the names of the authors and publishers. Send them a review copy and a persuasive cover letter suggesting why your book should be a resource or reference in future editions of their book.

Resource directories are useful as references. Search for directories appropriate to the market you are trying to reach. See *Directories in Print* by the Gale Group or *Guide to American Directories* by Todd Publications in the library.

"There is only one thing in the world worse than being talked about, and that is not being talked about."

- Oscar Wilde

A book stops selling when the author does.

4. Ways to Sell Your Books Direct

Many authors/publishers have made small fortunes selling books directly to readers, particularly with a title in a tightly defined market. However, very few titles come off the press as instant best sellers. Your book is a product, and like any other product it requires promotion. There are numerous ways to sell directly to the reader (and book trade). What works for one book may not work for another. With so many options, systematically test several promotional strategies to find what combination works best for you and your book. Realize that the author is the most important asset when it comes to selling books direct. No one knows more about the book than the author. Personal contact, a smile and an autograph often creates the goodwill which can lead to a sale. A more comprehensive description of ideas can be found in *1001 Ways to Market Your Book* by John Kremer and *Publish to Win* by Jerrold Jenkins & Anne Stanton.

> Have your distribution network in place before selling books to the public. This makes your book accessible to those who may purchase later.

• **Co-op Programs.** Co-op programs can help you stretch your promotional dollars. This happens when a group of people with similar interests or complementary products share the costs to reach their audience. This can reduce your expenses, but may dilute your message. Co-oping has many forms, including: mailings, advertising, catalog insertions and exhibits. Share with someone whose product blends with yours to reduce competing or conflicting messages.

Author Tours

An author tour can be a rewarding, though expensive, endurance test. It is one of the best ways to reach the book buying public in a relatively short period of time. Whether travelling by plane, train or RV, select your destinations at least 2 months in advance. Then, book appearances on as many TV and radio programs in each area as possible. Inform all bookstores of your promotional activity and encouraging them to have your book in stock. Identify the most popular bookstore in each location and give a lecture or reading followed by a booksigning. The libraries, community colleges and universities also offer speaking opportunities for touring authors. Send notices to the area's local daily and weekly newspapers outlining your activities. They may be interested in an interview with you or will mention you in their upcoming events section. Smaller communities and cities are a more inviting environment for less well-known authors. Your visit will compete with fewer events, often attracting larger audiences than you would in a major metropolitan area. Publicity opportunities are more accessible in smaller communities. Let your distributor or wholesalers know of your plans in advance, and many will print your tour schedule in their monthly bookstore mailer. (See the *Directory of Publications and Broadcast Media* for media listings in each city).

On national tours, consider paying for a listing in the *American Bookseller Association's* weekly newsletter: *Bookselling This Week* (800-637-0037) which publicizes author tours to member bookstores.

Hotel consolidators can book and discount hotel rates in many cities throughout the United States. Contact the following about their programs:

Hotel Reservation Network
8140 Walnut Hill Ln #203
Dallas TX 75231
(800) 715-7666
www.hoteldiscount.com

RMC Travel Center
424 Madison Ave #705
New York NY 10017
(800) 782-2674
www.rmcwebtravel.com

- **Book Signings.** Unless your event is backed by a great deal of media promotion, it is doubtful that people will be lined up waiting for your autograph. However, a book signing serves many purposes. Your book will be displayed in the store. You begin building relationships with the store owner, manager and staff (who can recommend your title to their customers) and you leave behind signed copies which increases the book's appeal. Most bookstores are receptive to signings because your presence helps to pull customers into their store, resulting in free publicity for both of you. There should be prior understanding of what the bookstore will do to promote your signing. Be prepared to send the local media advance notice of your signing as most will list this free of charge. Be creative during the signing to break the ice for hesitant onlookers. Wear a smile and have flyers to give to those who walk by. Perhaps a sign or a giveaway will help draw attention to your table. If appropriate, even dress up to match the persona of your book. Bring extra books in the event the bookstore does not have enough in stock. Be sure to make payment arrangements before using the books you brought. See the *American Book Trade Directory* in the library for a national listing of bookstores.

- ❏ **Book Signing Party.** Kick off the release of your book with a booksigning party at your home, office or the local bookstore. Gather friends, family, neighbors, associates, colleagues and anyone else who would support you and your book's message. Send invitations a month in advance, RSVP. Invite the local media. This is a celebration, make it fun. Do a reading or mini-workshop and have refreshments for the guests. This is a great time to sell books direct and set the tone for your bookselling adventure.

"To write a book is easy; it only requires pen and ink and the ever patient paper. To read a book is more difficult, because of the tendency to go to sleep... but the most difficult task of all that a mortal man can embark is to sell a book."
- Sir Stanley Unwin

Presentations

One of the most profitable times to sell books is after a speaking engagement. This may include seminars, workshops, lectures, media presentations, demonstrations or book readings. They can be conducted anywhere there is a willing audience. In addition to bookstores and libraries, social, civic and business organizations are all looking for speakers. Find a group to sponsor and promote your seminar to their members. This will help to offset any costs you incur and provide a built-in endorsement for you and your book. Most groups will let you sell directly to members after the presentation. Many cities have adult education programs at community colleges which welcome authors willing to conduct special workshops. View your presentation as a performance and plan accordingly. Use your knowledge to inform and entertain. Hone your speaking skills first in front of local civic clubs such as the Rotary, Lions or the Chamber of Commerce. Use an evaluation form asking what they liked or didn't like about your presentation helping to fine tune your message. As your speaking skills improve and your audience grows in size, consider using a Speaker's Bureau listed in the phone book. They are agents who market speakers for a percentage of the take. Contact the following trade association:

National Speakers Association
1500 S Priest Dr
Tempe AZ 85281
(480) 968-2552
www.nsaspeaker.org

❏ **More on Libraries.** In your travels, do not overlook libraries for generating publicity and reviews through presentations. Most public libraries have an events coordinator or "Friends of the Library" groups who organize author and fund raising activities and many allow you to sell your books direct. Often the library will order a copy or two for its own shelves.

One of the most important ingredients in a
recipe for speechmaking is plenty of shortening.

Exhibiting Books

Exhibiting books at a trade show, conference or festival is a great place to show, sell or introduce a title to a tightly targeted audience. When not attending an important show, find others to represent your title. Some shows have a combined exhibit area. For a small fee, your books and literature can be placed on a table along with other publishers. As an alternative, find another exhibitor or exhibitor service willing to include your book with its display.

❑ **Book Trade Shows.** The primary purpose of a regional, national or international book trade show is to introduce new titles to the publishing industry. When planned effectively, a trade show can be a powerful component of your marketing plan. Bookstore owners and Subsidiary Rights Agents will browse and make seasonal buying decisions. This is an ideal opportunity to win shelf space in bookstores or to sell foreign rights. Whether using a booth or table, orchestrate your space to encourage attendees to stop and browse.

• **Regional Book Trade Shows.** Many regional publishing, library and bookseller associations have book shows aimed at the book trade (and in some cases the public) with tables and booths available at far more reasonable rates than the national shows. Here you can make valuable contacts with the regional trade and network with nearby author/publishers. Perhaps these contacts can lead to combining marketing efforts at future shows. Call the American Booksellers Association (800) 637-0037 for a list of dates and locations of Regional Bookseller Associations Trade Shows. Your local bookstore can direct you to the regional bookseller association for your area. Contact PMA (310) 372-2732 for a listing of regional publishing associations and their shows.

• **National Book Trade Shows.** Book Expo America (formerly called the ABA Convention & Trade Exhibit) is North America's largest book event and occurs annually around the end of

May. This is a key time for publishers to display their new titles to the book trade and walk the floor to get a sense of what's new in the industry. The American Library Association's (ALA) annual event occurs around the end of June and is the premier place to meet buyers from libraries around the country. Inquire about ALA's divisional conferences which include the public and school library conferences.

Book Expo America	**American Library Association**
383 Main Ave	50 E Huron St
Norwalk CT 06851	Chicago IL 60611
(800) 840-5614	(800) 545-2433
www.reedexpo.com	www.ala.org

• **International Book Trade Shows.** Frankfurt & London Book Fairs have the largest book fairs in Europe, drawing attendance from around the world. If you cannot attend, the following organizations will display, and even negotiate foreign rights for you, through their staffed exhibits. PMA and SPAN offer book exhibit services as well. *See page 19.*

International Publishers Alliance	**International Titles / Harry Smith**
9200 Sunset Blvd # 404	931 E 56th St
Los Angeles CA 90069	Austin TX 78751
(800) 966-7716	(512) 451-2221

❏ **Other Trade Shows & Conventions.** Each market niche has its own trade show or convention. These can be great places to make valuable contacts and get exposure within an industry. In a world of impersonal sales practices, face-to-face interaction is hard to beat. Assembled in one place is a high concentration of potential buyers and industry leaders. Clearly define what you hope to gain from the event and plan your space accordingly. Take into consideration the cost of travel, food and lodging as they can quickly absorb profits from direct sales. See the *Encyclopedia of Associations* and *Trade Show Worldwide* in the library. The Chamber of Commerce or the local Convention Center will know who is holding meetings and conventions are being held in your vicinity.

❑ **Specialty Conferences.** Individual promoters and organizations sponsor conferences and expositions around the country, focusing on very specific subject interests. Often these conferences travel from place to place bringing a group of popular authors and presenters speaking on the conference subject. Contact the sponsors to make your speaking expertise available, particularly when held in your area. If you cannot attend, ask who will be managing the book sales for the conference. Contact that person and suggest your title be included.

❑ **Book Festivals.** Exhibiting at a major book fair can be extremely profitable, yet an exhausting experience lasting a weekend and sometimes longer. These fairs offer opportunities to sell your books directly to the public for list price. Have a visually appealing exhibit and a well conceived plan that draws attention to your books in this highly competitive environment. Offer your expertise. Most bookfairs have author readings, lectures and panel discussions.

The number of books to bring is gauged by the estimated attendance. For example: If attendance is projected at 30,000, figure each person will spend an average of $10, thus $300,000 will be spent at the fair. Divide that total by the number of exhibitors (say 250) and your take could be $1200. Subtract your travel expenses and the entrance fee to assess if it is time well spent. Listed below are a few of the country's largest book fairs:

Miami Bookfair International
Miami-Dade Community College
300 NE Second Ave #1515
Miami FL 33132
(305) 237-3258
www.miamibookfair.com

LA Times Festival of Books
Times Mirror Square
Los Angeles CA 90053
(800) 528-4637 x72665
www.latimes.com/festivalofbooks

Northwest Bookfest
3131 Western Ave #411
Seattle WA 98121
(206) 378-1883
www.nwbookfest.org

Rocky Mountain Book Festival
Colorado Center for the Book
2123 Downing St
Denver CO 80205
(303) 839-8320
www.coloradobook.org

NY is Book Country
c/o HarperCollins Publishing
10 E 53rd St
New York NY 10022
(212) 207-7270
www.nyisbookcountry.com

❏ **Other Festivals & Fairs.** Local sponsors promote special interest festivals or summer art and street fairs. These can be excellent forums for showing and selling your book direct. Author appearances can draw local media attention, and become publicity vehicles. Check the library or bookstores for books on local events, then contact the sponsors and request an exhibitors package. Calculate your break-even point before paying for space.

> To reduce your exhibiting costs,
> consider co-oping with another author/publisher.

❏ **Gift Shows.** If the gift market is a target for your book, there is no better place to display your title than at a gift show. Assembled in one location are all the key players including reps, suppliers, media, manufacturers and distributors; a superb place to meet others interested in carrying or distributing your book. The focus is on seasonal purchasing. Winter and Summer being the major buying seasons as orders are taken well in advance. Before the show, think about mailing a flyer to all the gift stores in the area announcing your attendance and booth number. Below are some the major gift shows and their phone numbers:

Atlanta	(404) 220-3000	www.americasmart.com
Chicago	(312) 527-4141	www.merchandisemart.com
Dallas	(214) 655-6100	www.dallasmarketcenter.com
Los Angeles	(213) 749-7911	www.lamart.com
New York	(212) 686-1203	www.41madison.com
San Francisco	(415) 861-7733	www.gcjm.com
Seattle	(206) 767-6800	www.seattlegiftcenter.com

Advertising

After you have exhausted all other means of publicity, turn to paid advertising. It comes in many forms, although advertising's intent remains the same; to motivate a favorable response from its audience. Advertising involves presenting the right product to the right audience with the right message at the right time. This is done by developing an ad that gains the reader's favorable attention, holds it long enough to get the intended message across, and then motivates a desired response.

It is difficult to know where to invest your advertising dollar. Begin by looking at ads in trade magazines to see what they are advertising, and how, and for design and layout ideas. Have your purpose clearly in mind when designing an ad. It may be to elicit a call, an inquiry, a visit or a sale. Draft every line, every word and every graphic with this purpose in mind. Focus on the readers' interests, as they want to know how your book will help them to gain, save, do or become something. Before making a sizable investment, start small and measure the effectiveness of your message. Use separate codes on each ad to track what works and what doesn't. Adjust your ad accordingly until it yields the best results. Determine which sources bring the highest response. Two general rules for advertising success are **timing** and **repetition**. See *How to Market a Product for Under $500* by Jeffrey Dobkins and *Words That Sell* by Richard Bayan. In the library, see *Standard Rate and Data* for a listing of periodicals and their advertising rates.

❑ **Space Advertising.** Space advertising involves placing an advertisement or insert in newspapers, catalogs, directories, newsletters, magazines, books or any supplement which targets your audience. Many publications have remnant space for sale. This is unsold advertising space, purchased at a discount. Most ad rates are negotiable despite what rate cards says. Factors such as ad positioning, advance payment and test rates for first time advertisers can all be utilized to negotiate better terms. Some publications will even trade an ad for a percentage of sales. To simplify your advertising purchasing requirements, search the phone book under media buyers or media placements companies.

> Radio ads are not a common method to advertise books. Radio requires frequent repetition for best results, thus the return may not exceed the cost.

• **Advertising to the Book Trade.** The release of your title could be announced to the book trade by advertising in a publishing trade magazine such as: Publishers Weekly, American Bookseller and Library Journal. Regional bookseller associations and book wholesalers also offer advertising specials to reach regional book buyers.

• **Classified Ads**. A classified ad is one of the least expensive forms of advertising. Do not use classified ads to sell so much as to compile a good mailing list or to test market the pull of an ad. A mailing list compiled from classified responses could yield high numbers of orders. Offer free information in return for a self-addressed, stamped envelope (SASE). Follow this up by sending an article, flyer, brochure or promotional material that encourages a purchase. Again, code ads to keep track of what works and what doesn't. The classified's are good for testing the readers response to a magazine or newspaper ad before you make a sizable investment in space advertising.

"Half the money I spend on advertising is a waste; the trouble is, I don't know which half."

- John Wanamaker

❑ **Direct Mail Advertising.** It is easier to sell books by direct mail if you can accurately identify and locate your audience or niche. Direct mail is quick to produce. You can plan, prepare and mail a small direct mail promotion in days. With the correct list, offer and sales copy, direct mail can be an efficient and lucrative way to reach your audience. Ask yourself: Is the product suitable for direct mail? Who is the target? Am I prepared to handle the incoming mail response, or should you use a fulfillment service? Associations and magazines generally rent a mailing list of their members or subscribers. See the *Encyclopedia of Associations* and the *Standard Directory of Periodicals* in the library for a listing of national associations and publications.

A profitable direct mail campaign requires a test run. Check your audience's response by mailing varied messages in small quantities and monitoring the results. Expect a 0 to 2% response rate until all the elements of the ad are refined and working together. Once you find a winning message and responsive list, just keep mailing. Use repetition by sending multiple messages to your audience either through ads or additional direct mailing. Typically, several repetitions and proper timing of the idea, product or service are required to convince buyers of their need. The most successful mail order campaign brings the most orders at the lowest possible cost.

Prerequisite for a Successful Direct Mail Campaign

1. Establish a clear purpose.
2. Target the appropriate audience.
3. Design the mailer to spell out the benefits.
4. Present the information in a clear, persuasive manner.
5. Test the effectiveness of the mailing list and mailer copy.
6. Make it easy for people to respond.

Direct mail advertising works best with books that are tightly targeted and have a retail price above $40 to offset mailing costs and still be profitable. An exception is when using your own list of past customers. Less expensive books can benefit from cooperative mailings by combining mailers with someone else's, thus sharing expenses. This reduces your mailing costs, but dilute your message and perhaps the response rate.

❏ **Elements of Direct Mail Advertising.** Direct mail advertising is an art and a science requiring that all elements work together to produce the best result. Each direct mail ad consist of four distinct elements:

• **The List:** The better your list, the better your success. Mailing to the wrong address or using an old list will ensure your mailing fails. Addresses change at about 20% per year. Purchase a clean list with a guarantee on the number of nixies (returns). Your own mailing list will usually yield the best return as existing customers are more inclined to respond than new customers.

> Good copy writing is lean. Simplify ads, letters and brochures by removing adjectives and adverbs that don't add power to the message. It's similar to cutting the fat off a steak: the nourishment and flavor remain, yet there is enough marbling to keep it juicy.

• **The Enclosure: (Letter/Brochure/Post Card).** Whether you use a letter, brochure, post card or any combination of these, the enclosure is the most important element in selling your message. It presents the benefits of owning and using your book. Have your primary objective clearly in mind. Do you want to motivate a call, an inquiry, a visit or an order? List the features and the benefits of your book and support your claims with testimonials. Give the facts (features): size, price and weight of the product. Benefits are what the product will do for the reader. Remember, when writing ad copy: features tell, benefits sell. Effective direct mail copy is tricky to write. Hire a professional when help is needed.

The debate about the use of long or short sales letters still ensues. The key lies in making the letter persuasive enough to move people to action. Use clear, plain and simple language. Make the message interesting and easy to read. An effective mailer is designed to engage the attention, interest and desire of the readers, and prompt them to action. Support your enclosures with testimonials, examples or statistics to convince the reader of its value. Post cards are a most economical way to mail because you get first class postage at a post card rate. However, the size limits the extent of the message.

> Hand address envelopes get opened more frequently than labeled envelopes. First class stamps often pull better than bulk rate. The difference in pull rate may outweigh the increased cost of postage. Test all variations before making a substantial investment.

• **The Envelope:** The envelope is like a store front, the first thing people see. Enticing people to open and read the enclosure is the objective. Make the envelope treatment the main decision in a mailing program. Whatever printed promise or teaser you present on the envelope, fulfill it in the enclosure.

• **The Reply:** The easiest response to get is a phone call. With a toll-free 800/888 number, prospective buyers can call to inquire about, or order your book. Offer an incentive to purchase now: a free gift, special report or discount. Make it convenient for people by using several response vehicles, such as: toll-free numbers, fax, credit card acceptance, e-mail or regular mail including a postage paid reply envelope.

❑ **Mailing Lists.** When renting mailing lists, be specific about your target audience. The more you can pin point your potential buyers, the higher your response rate. In addition to the companies listed below, contact government agencies, catalog companies, associations, manufacturers and publishers who sell to your market about their mailing lists. Below are companies which specialize in renting or selling lists and address labels to book publishers. Request list types and pricing from the following:

American Booksellers Association
828 S Broadway
Tarrytown NY 10591
(800) 637-0037
www.bookweb.org

Bradley Communications Corp
135 E Plumstead Ave
Landsdowne PA 19050
(800) 989-1400
www.rtir.com

Cahners Direct Mail Service
1350 E Touhy Ave
Des Plaines IL 60018
(800) 323-4958
www.cahners.com

American Business Lists
5711 S 86th Cr
Omaha NE 68127
(800) 336-8349
www.infousa.com

Para-Lists by Poynter
Box 8206
Santa Barbara CA 93118
(805) 968-7277
www.parapublishing.com

Open Horizons
Box 205
Fairfield IA 52556
(800) 796-6130
www.bookmarket.com

Record all orders and inquiries for your own mailing list. Your house list can be a source of income, if leased. Periodic mailings to people on your mailing list provides chances for updating addresses and for keeping in contact with customers.

❏ **Card Packs.** Card packs are a collection of loose post cards bundled together in one mailing. This is co-op type advertising. There are card packs for nearly any audience. However, the message may be diluted with many other cards competing for the readers' attention. This form of advertising has an extremely low response rate, but it is one of the least expensive forms of direct mailing. The following company offers card pack services and a free directory of 100 card pack publishers upon request:

Solar Communications
1120 Frontenac Rd
Naperville IL 60563
(800) 323-2751
www.leaderofthepack.com

The Internet

The World Wide Web on the Internet is the most important new communication medium since TV. It is a rapidly growing marketplace for the sale of books. The following are common ways to promote and sell books using the Internet:

❏ **Web Site.** A Web Site is essentially a storefront on the World Wide Web that people can visit via computers. It acts as an introduction, to you, your book(s) and your publishing venture using a collection of information presented in words, sounds and images. A Web Site can include promotional programs, such as: new book announcements, press releases, book reviews, author tour schedules, excerpts, graphics of book covers, ordering information and even links to services at other Web locations. When people visit your site, they may order, print or request additional information on your products or services. The following company specializes in the development of Web Sites for book publishers:

BookZone, Inc.
Box 9642
Scottsdale AZ 85252
(800) 536-6162
www.bookzone.com

❏ **Promoting Your Web Site.** Establishing an Internet presence is not enough. An active promotional strategy to attract people to your site is essential. To make the most of this new technology, an effective promotional strategy might include:

- Getting listed in search engines and directories.
- Establishing reciprocal links.
- Creating site promotional activities.
- Using push technology.
- Getting involved on mailing lists.
- Participating in newsgroups.

• **Search Engines and Directories**. Let your audience know your site and books exist. An important way is to register your site in the online indexes that most people use to find things on the Web. There are hundreds of search engines and directories, so be selective to best reach your audience. The top eight search engines are:

- Yahoo	www.yahoo.com
- Excite	www.excite.com
- Infoseek	www.infoseek.com
- HotBot	www.hotbot.com
- LookSmart	www.looksmart.com
- Lycos	www.lycos.com
- AltaVista	www.altavista.com
- Dogpile	www.dogpile.com

Visit WebStep 100 (www.mmgexpress.com) for a ranking of the top 100 places to be listed and assistance in submitting your site to them. You can also conduct your own search by using search engine advanced options, and search for your book's specialty *plus* the word *search engines* or *indices* or *directories.*

• **Reciprocal Links.** Exchanging links with other sites that attract the same audience is one of the most effective ways to promote your site and books. You place a link to their site (from yours) and they do the same. Send an e-mail requesting an exchange. It's often easier to first establish a link to other sites, then ask for a link to yours.

• **Creating Site Promotional Activities.** What can you do to attract people to your site? In addition to offering excerpts of your book(s), consider sponsoring a contest, offering special prices, presenting special information, giving free reports, allowing people to ask questions about the subject of your books. Anything that can be done to bring visitors to your site will generate interest in your books.

• **Using Push Technology.** This refers to an automatic content or information delivery system. For example, people can request to be on your electronic mailing list from which they receive a weekly or monthly e-mail newsletter or subject update automatically. If you collect e-mail addresses, let visitors know how you will be using them, as many people are sensitive about how their address is used.

• **Getting Involved on Mailing Lists.** Subscribing to mailing lists, which are sometimes called *listserves* is a popular way to connect with people interested in the subject of your book. This is a great way to meet and exchange e-mails with people who have similar interests. Everyone who is interested sends an e-mail to a specific address, and then all messages are sent to everyone on the list. Mailing lists, in fact, are a simple type of push technology because they send information automatically to the list members.

Most mailing lists do not permit advertising. However, offering help or answering questions from interested parties is a way to mention your book. Most e-mail programs allow you to attach a signature or short file of information, at the bottom of each message that can tell about your book. If your program does not have a signature capability, create a four or five line text file and cut and paste it onto the bottom of every e-mail you send. Before subscribing, spend a little time getting acquainted with the list before taking part.

• **Participating in Newsgroups.** Newsgroups are another way people with similar interests get together. While mailing lists send messages to subscribers by e-mail, newsgroup members must go to the group's location on the Internet's Usenet. Again, use your program's signature capability at the bottom of your message to let people know about your products, services and site location. As with mailing lists, check it out before participating. Newsgroup subject directories can be found at: www.dejanews.com

❑ **Online Author Interviews.** To book an appearance, contact the online host by e-mail and present your credentials. America Online has a center stage auditorium where they book headliners. Prodigy has a similar venue. Remember, Online services such as AOL and Prodigy can only be accessed by members. You might find a more receptive audience in smaller special interest newsgroups. Inkspot (www.inkspot.com) holds forums in their Book Cafe. Sometimes promotion is weak or nonexistent. Announce your own appearance by posting in appropriate discussion groups, offering a free transcript upon request to those who can't attend.

❑ **Miscellaneous Book Marketing Contacts.** The following are additional marketing and publishing resources on the Internet:

• **Bookwire: www.bookwire.com** Bookwire is a comprehensive and easily used guide to book resources on the Internet. It has more than 3,500 links to book related sites around the world.

• **Book Marketing Online.** This is John Kremer's site, author of *1001 Ways to Market Your Book*. Receive a free weekly book marketing update by sending an e-mail to majordomo@bookzone.com and type in the message area: subscribe bmu

• **Publishers Marketing Association's Mail List.** This is a forum of publishers who share ideas and answer questions for list members. Be prepared to receive over 100 e-mails a day covering a wide array of publishing topics. To join, send an e-mail to listserv@hslc.org and type in the message block SUBSCRIBE PMA-L with your first and last name.

A Final Thought. Marketing a book can be a daunting task with a multitude of options and decisions. This emphasizes the importance of a well conceived marketing plan to provide focus and direction. After your book's initial release, apply the "one a day" rule by doing something *every day* to support your book's sales effort. Make a phone call, secure an interview, set up a speaking engagement or send out a review copy. The key is persistence over time. As the famous riddle goes: How do you eat an elephant? One bite at a time. **Good Luck!**

Appendix and Indexes

Sample Terms & Conditions (for Special Sales)

Title: A Simple Guide To Marketing Your Book

Subtitle: What An Author And Publisher Can Do
                      To Sell More Books

Author: Mark Ortman

Description: The easiest way to prepare and organize your book
                      marketing efforts. A step-by-step handbook that
                      includes: how to get started, where to find the best
                      places for distributing and the many ways to create
                      a demand for your book.

ISBN: 0-9634699-4-0

Retail Price: $9.95 Softcover

Size/Weight: 5.5 x 8.5 / 93 pages / 5.5 ounces each

Shipping: F.O.B. Bellingham WA 98226
                      Free shipping on prepaid orders

Discounts | 5-23 copies | 40% |
Direct From | 24-99 | 50% |
Publisher | 100-499 | 55% |
                     | 500+ | Call for quote |

Terms: Net 30 with approved credit.

New Accounts: Furnish 3 trade references, one bank reference
                      including the name and phone number
                      of their individual in charge of accounts payable.
                      Please include your resale/tax number.

To Order: Phone (360) 671-5858

Trade Orders: Baker & Taylor • INGRAM • Partner's West

News Release Layout

Use Your Letterhead

NEWS RELEASE   Contact Name
                                            Phone Number

For Immediate Release
Date (for time sensitive material, list specific kill date)

HEADER STATEMENT
(A good headline succinctly summarizes the information to follow.)

In the body of the news release, write a one or two page,

double spaced message in 200 words or less. Keep to

the facts and answer throughout the release WHO,

WHAT, WHEN, WHERE, WHY and HOW about

the author, event or book.

When writing a release for your book, include availability,

Publisher, the ISBN number and retail price.

Signal the end of the release with the number sign
typed three times (###) or three astericks (***) or the
word END.

###

Marketing Plan Questionnaire

1. Budget   HOW much will be spent?

How will I allocate my budget?

- Postage and Supplies
- Review Copy Giveaways
- Printed Promotional Matter
- Advertising
- Travel
- Miscellaneous

2. Product   WHAT is being sold?

What is the main message or theme?

Why is that message or theme important?

Describe the book in one paragraph.

How is it unique?

Realistic strengths and weaknesses of the book?

By reading the book, what will the reader:

Gain?
Save?
Do?
Become?

Write an author biography which may include:

- Why the book was written?
- Education and professional training.
- Prizes, honors and awards earned.
- Membership in professional associations.
- Specific qualifications for writing this book.
- Circumstances connected with the book that
  might have news value.

3. Audience   WHO will buy your book and WHERE will you find them?

Who would benefit from the book's information?
Who are the key opinion leaders on the subject?
Where is the audience found?

- Membership affiliation (clubs, associations)
- Conferences and Trade Show's they attend
- Catalogs they may receive by mail
- Newsletters and periodicals they read
- Places they shop
- Media formats they read, watch and listen to
- Which companies, organizations, associations could use the book as a premium giveaway

4. Distribution   WHERE will the book be made available?

Where are similar books being sold?
Who would sell the book along with their product or service?
Where can this book be made available to the audience?

❏ Academic Markets	❏ Government
❏ Associations	❏ Gift Market
❏ Book Clubs	❏ Internet
❏ Bookstores	❏ Libraries
❏ Catalogs	❏ Premium and Incentive
❏ Corporations	❏ Specialty Retail Outlets
❏ Foreign Markets	❏ TV Shopping Networks
❏ Fund raisers	❏ Warehouse Clubs

What will I do to convince each channel of distribution to carry my book?

5. Promotion   WHAT will be done to create a demand?

How can the book be publicized?

- ❏ Book Reviews
- ❏ Media Appearances
- ❏ Targeted Book Giveaways
- ❏ Articles submitted to Print Media
- ❏ Listings in Other Publications
- ❏ Other

How will a demand for the book be created?

- ❏ Advertisements
- ❏ Author Tour
- ❏ Direct Mail
- ❏ Internet
- ❏ Presentations
- ❏ Trade Shows
- ❏ Other

Who can be asked to endorse or provide a testimonial?

6. Timing   WHEN will each idea be implemented?

The publication date is?
Before the publication date, what must be done?
After the publication date, what must be done?

*"The writing of a best-seller represents only a fraction
of the total effort required to create one."*
- Ted Nicholas

Regional Book Wholesalers

Before sending a book, inquire about submission requirements. A complete list of specialty book wholesalers and distributors can be found in the *American Book Trade Directory* in the library.

Bookazine Co
75 Hook Rd
Bayonne NJ 07002
(201) 339-7777
www.bookazine.com

Bookmen Inc
525 N Third St
Minneapolis MN 55401
(612) 341-3333
www.bookmen@bookmen.com

BookPeople
7900 Edgewater Dr
Oakland CA 94621
(510) 632-4700
www.bponline.com

Booksource
1230 Macklind Ave
St Louis MO 63110
(314) 647-0600
www.booksource.com

Brodart Co
500 Arch St
Williamsport PA 17705
(800) 233-8467
www.brodart.com

the distributors
702 S Michigan
South Bend IN 46601
(219) 232-8500

Koen Book Distributors
10 Twosome Dr
Moorestown NJ 08057
(800) 257-8481
www.koen.com

Koen Pacific Distributors
18249 Olympic Ave So
Tukwila WA 98188
(206) 575-7544
www.koenpacific.com

New Leaf Distribution Co
401 Thorton Rd
Lithia Springs GA 30122
(770) 948-7845
www.newleaf-dist.com

Partners Book Distribution Inc
2325 Jarco Dr
Holt MI 48842
(517) 694-3205

Partners West Book Distributing
1901 Raymond Ave SW #C
Renton WA 98055
(425) 227-8486

Southern Book Services Inc
5154 NW 165th St
Hialeah FL 33014
(305) 624-4545
www.southernbook.com

Organization & Reference Index

Subject Index

Books by Mark Ortman

Simple Guide to Self-Publishing
A Step-By-Step Handbook To Prepare, Print, Distribute & Publish
Your Own Book
An award-winning handbook to guide you through the publishing process. Filled with money-saving ideas and checklists, this book includes: how to get started, phone numbers and addresses of key industry contacts, who will print your book for less and the many ways to distribute and sell your book. 64p / ISBN 0-9634699-0-8 / **$9.95**

Simple Guide to Marketing Your Book
What An Author And Publisher Can Do To Sell More Books
A concise step-by-step planning guide to make marketing your book easier. Includes: the six steps to a marketing plan, how to define your audience, where to find the best places to distribute your book, how to promote your book on the internet and more. 93p / ISBN 0-9634699-4-0 / **$10.95**

Now That Makes Sense!
Relating To People With Wit And Wisdom
An entertaining look at communication. This collection is filled with quips, quotes, perusals and wisdom by history's wittiest minds. A perfect reference for speakers, writers, newsletter editors or anyone who works with people. 223p / ISBN 0-9634699-9-1 **$11.95**

The Teacher's Book of Wit
Quips, Quotes And Anecdotes To Make Learning More Fun
A winning collections of quips, quotes, anecdotes and humorous definitions to make teaching and learning more fun. Ideal for the classroom, lectures, homeschooling, presentations and reports. 95p / ISBN 0-9634699-7-5 / **$9.95**

To order, send check or money order in US funds to:

WISE OWL BOOKS
Box 29205
Bellingham WA 98228
(360) 671-5858
www.wise**owl**books.com/publish

Shipping: $3.00 per order shipping in the United States
WA State residents include 7.8% Sales Tax

About the Author

Author, publisher and workshop leader **Mark Ortman** received a Bachelor's Degree in Marketing and a Master's Degree in Communication. He spent twelve years working in the training and development field, and was the recipient of nine national instructional awards for his inspiring teaching style. Currently, he lectures, conducts workshops, consults and coaches authors/publishers through the publishing process. His published works include *Now That Makes Sense! Relating to People With Wit and Wisdom, So Many Ways To Say Thank You, The Teacher's Book Of Wit,* the award-winning *Simple Guide to Self-Publishing* and *A Simple Guide to Marketing Your Book.* He also plays keyboards and has released *Wednesday's Dream*, an album of instrumental music. He lives in the Pacific Northwest.

Invite Mark to speak at your next meeting,
conference or special event.
Phone (360) 671-5858